LEARN TO
PAINT & DRAW

Published by Igloo Books Limited
Cottage Farm
Mears Ashby Road
Sywell
Northants
NN6 0BJ
info@igloo-books.com

This edition published 2007

Project management: Talking Design

Editorial and design management: Emma Hayley and Jenny Ross
Coordinator: Adam Phillips
Authors and illustrators: Sarah Green and Chris Christoforou
Cover and text design: Paul Barton
Layout: Kurt Young
Additional illustrations: Peter J Green (John) and Carolyn Green
Photography: Daley Rowner, Derwent, Photos.com
With thanks to Victoria Chow

LEARN TO
PAINT & DRAW

From a Simple Sketch To a Beautiful Painting

Contents

Part 1 – Learn to Draw

Part 2 – Learn to Paint

Learn to Draw

An Introduction to Drawing

Learning to draw is a very rewarding experience. You will be able to capture moments forever, express thoughts and feelings, and learn to become more observant about the world that surrounds you.

An Artist's First Step

Most of us have some experience of art, normally from formal education. Once we leave school, we tend to leave any practice of art behind too. If you have ever wondered if you really could learn to draw, or rediscover any childhood talent, then this book is for you. It will guide you gently through all the main elements that any budding artist needs to create successful compositions. There will be simple-to-follow exercises which will teach basic rules of composition and perspective, as well as how to tackle specific subjects, such as landscapes and portraits.

The emphasis will be on learning to master basic techniques in pencil drawing, as well as guidance on how to apply colour using different drawing mediums.

You will learn how to use a sketchbook to collect ideas and inspiration for pictures, as well as act as a practicing tool. All the exercises will gradually build your confidence to allow you to develop your own style and get creating beautiful pictures. There will be lots of tips on how to begin mastering simple techniques that, over time and with practice, will give you excellent foundation drawing skills. Above all, you will have fun and learn new skills which will give you a lifetime of pleasure.

- Follow the step-by-step examples of methods and techniques that will help develop confidence and ability.

- Learn how to use a sketchbook to practice techniques, collect reference material, and begin creating original compositions.

- Discover how to use different drawing materials to create a range of textures and tonal qualities which will add perspective and atmosphere to any drawing.

- Understand the importance of careful planning when creating a composition by using a simple checklist.

- Begin to master perspective and proportion to create the illusion of three-dimensional space within a composition.

- Learn about the range of drawing materials and equipment that are available and how to select the most appropriate for your needs.

*Rediscover the joys of
drawing and learn how
to make the most of
your creativity*

Why Learn to Draw?

Learning to draw can seem a daunting prospect, as there are so many different things to think about before you even put pencil to paper. However, everyone has the physical ability to be able to draw – children will automatically make marks on paper and begin to express themselves and the world that surrounds them long before they can write.

Drawings have been found in prehistoric caves which were used as a rudimentary form of communication long before language and writing came about. Drawing is one of the fundamental things that humans use to convey emotion and capture a sense of time.

A drawing can be as simple as a series of marks on any surface that conveys some kind of message or emotion, or an incredibly technically complicated, emotionally expressive statement.

Drawings have many functions and can be made in limitless ways – the only restriction is the artist's imagination. A drawing can be made from a pencil on paper, but it can also be created from

other mediums, even paint. There is a crossover between the two disciplines of drawing and painting – in fact it is virtually impossible to paint without having drawing skills. Many other craft-based techniques rely on a simple grasp of drawing in one way or another draughtsmen, architects and designers all need to draw when developing concepts. Even computers use basic drawing principles in many graphic-based disciplines such as layout and website design.

- It is important to learn how to judge when a drawing is complete. Many people find drawing a challenge because they believe they have to produce a direct representation of whatever it is they are looking at but, in most cases, a good drawing is as much about what is left out as to that which is captured on the paper. A good artist will learn, often through trial and error, just what can be left out to create a visually stimulating piece. There is nothing to prevent an artist from interpreting a scene in any way that they feel will benefit the overall composition.

This book will help you to interpret any subject in a spontaneous and fresh way, which will give feeling and meaning to your drawings.

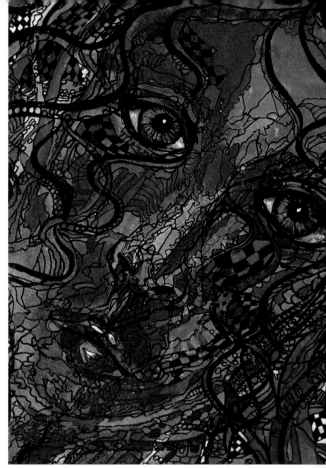

Drawing does not have to produce a direct representation of what you see – through trial and error, you will find a style that works for you

Defining Drawing

Remember, a drawing is a series of marks that convey emotions and meanings. A good drawing is one that works on this level, as opposed to a technically superior composition that lacks depth and understanding of the subject.

After all, a drawing is an interpretation of the subject as the artist views it. Each artist will, through practice, begin to develop a feeling of individuality as they discover their own style.

Some people draw because it is the beginning of a longer process – for example, when composing a painting. Yet drawing is an art form in its own right. There are many artists who choose drawing as their main type of creative expression. Either way, there are certain things to consider before you begin. If you decide to make an objective drawing then you will be looking to create a representational, or "lifelike," composition. This will create a fairly accurate, factually informative piece of work. A subjective drawing will be far more expressive, with more passion and feeling, which may even result in a very abstract composition.

Most good artists are able to find a balance between these two types of drawing. There will be times when an objective approach is the best option, especially if it is to record certain details of a time and a place, or as a reference, such as when planning a painting or other type of art form. This does not mean that there should be no hint of expression, as even an objective composition needs to have life and feeling within it to be engaging. At other times, a subjective, free-flowing drawing may still rely on some objective elements to make sure that the work can be easily interpreted.

Another consideration is what type of drawing medium should be used for each kind of drawing. Much of this will be determined by the effect that you wish to create, although some types of drawing material will be harder to use in certain situations. This will be one of the things that will come with practice. You will understand through trial and error, which materials work best. By the end of this book, you will have a clear understanding of the types of materials available and which are the best methods of applying them to your drawing.

If you feel inspired by a subject, then you are halfway to creating a successful composition. Most drawings work because the artist has been able to connect with the subject. You may have a favourite subject that you wish to concentrate on, such as landscape painting or still life flowers. It is worth attempting other styles and mediums from time to time as this will prevent you from becoming stale and may even give a fresh perspective on your favourite subject. Trying new things can be daunting, but challenging yourself as an artist is exciting and you may discover that you have talents that you never thought were there.

There is no such thing as a right way to draw; rather there are techniques that can be used to help you gain confidence as an artist, and even these can be manipulated to create new visual effects as your confidence grows.

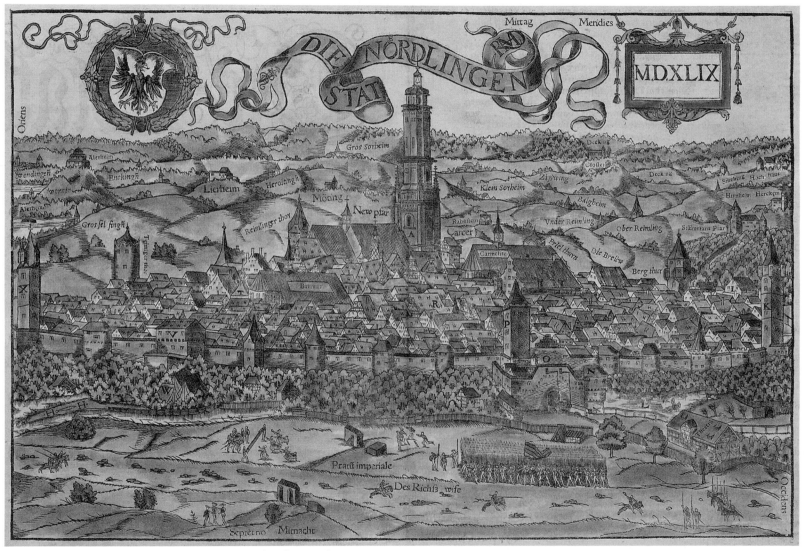

Mastering the art of drawing is both a demanding but hugely rewarding pursuit

13

For the beginner, it can be frustrating to see how some people can seemingly pick up a pencil and create a work of art with hardly any effort. A blank piece of paper appears to hold no fear for them as they dash off a brilliant drawing.

Introduction to Planning your Drawing

While these types of artists seem to have a natural talent, it does not mean that they are not making a series of decisions about their drawing before and while they create it. It is just that they are so comfortable with the process that it seems that they are doing very little.

Any artist should have a mental checklist that they go through before embarking on a drawing. Careful planning will mean that you are more likely to produce a piece of work that is satisfying and does what you set out to achieve. Depending on the type of drawing you require, you will need to decide on a range of factors which will influence the end result; subject matter, timescale and materials are all crucial things to consider during the initial planning stage.

Things to think about when planning a drawing

• What do you want your drawing to "say?" What visual impact do you want your drawing to have and how do you hope to achieve it? Decide on an objective or subjective approach. Is your drawing for research? If so, an objective viewpoint is best. If you want to portray emotion or the feel of a specific place, object or event, then be more subjective.

• What will be the best drawing medium to achieve the effect you want? Think about the practicalities, such as: will the drawing be done on location? What level of detail will your drawing contain? Certain types of drawing medium will be more suited to finer detail, such as pencils and pens, whereas charcoal, pastels, and chalk will give a more fluid, expressive feeling and can quickly capture the essence of a subject – all these will be described in more detail in the "materials and equipment" section of this book.

• Have you done sufficient research? Are you working from memory or photographs, or are you on location? If you are collecting data for a composition then how will you record all the relevant information? Will you be using a sketchbook? Perhaps you need to make additional notes or do several sketches from different viewpoints. Maybe you should do a range of drawings; some subjective, to capture the mood; others more objective, to ensure you include all the relevant details you require for any final composition – you will learn how to create and use a sketchbook later in this book.

• How are you going to apply the image to the paper? Will you be working in "landscape" or "portrait?" What viewpoint will you be taking? All these questions will be dealt with in the next section of the book.

As you become more confident with drawing, you will find that these types of considerations will become second nature to you. Don't worry if you make a few mistakes along the way, or forget to do certain things. You will always learn from anything that goes wrong – in fact, you may even achieve some fantastic results by attempting to experiment a little.

Creating your composition

What makes a good composition? It can be hard to say exactly why we think one drawing is better composed than another – often it is just because it "feels" right. As you get more experienced at creating your own, you will begin to recognize those elements that can really improve a drawing.

Composition is the way in which an artist designs and organizes a picture in relation to the space available. It should be determined by the elements that you want your picture to include mood, atmosphere, and impact, as well as the actual subject matter.

If a drawing is well composed, then it will invite the eye in and allow it to eventually rest in the centre of the composition, after having taken in the whole picture. The edges of the picture act as the frame, so it is important not to over-emphasize the outer area, as this will distract from the rest of the composition.

- An important consideration is the use of space within a composition. Each object and space within a picture bear a direct relation to each other – these are called "positive" and "negative" spaces. For example, in a landscape, the positive space would be the objects: trees, hills, buildings, clouds, etc. The negative space is the areas between the objects. If these elements are successfully interwoven, then the composition will be successful.

- Using contrast also improves a composition. For example, to emphasize how dominant something is, place a small object next to it – light/dark; thick/thin; shadow/light.

- Keep your picture balanced – if you draw attention to one side then the rhythm of the picture will be distorted and it will appear unbalanced. Always try to keep the eye stimulated enough to explore the picture, without it becoming distracted.

Composition is the foundation of any good drawing

- Think of an element within the whole composition, which will act as the focal point – something for the eye to finally be drawn to. This will normally be of some significance to the picture as a whole; perhaps this object or person will help the artist to reflect the meaning of the piece. Remember not to place it too centrally as the eye will naturally go direct to that point. Instead, try leading the eye around the picture by making the composition as interesting as possible.

- Don't place objects in rows as this could make your picture appear lifeless and boring. Vary the viewpoint to create more movement around the picture and give it greater depth.

The Golden Mean

Most drawings and paintings are done on rectangular paper or canvas. As a general rule, landscape (including skyscape, seascape, and townscape) compositions are created with the long edge of the paper or canvas as the horizontal line, whereas portrait compositions use the long edge as the vertical as this best suits the shape of the human body and face. However, as with everything in art, you are at liberty to experiment with these norms.

It is not advisable to place objects within a picture too close to the centre of a composition, or split it centrally, either vertically or horizontally, as this will lead the eye directly to the mid point and the rest of the picture will be lost.

When using these rectangular, horizontal or vertical canvases, the usual rule is that you apply the Golden Mean or Golden Ratio principle when composing the layout of your picture. This means dividing up a rectangle using geometry which was devised by Renaissance painters, who believed it was the most perfect layout.

It is based on the mathematical relationship between three points on a straight line in which the ratio AC:BC equals the ratio BC:AC. If that sounds confusing, a simpler way of describing it is that any picture should be divided up by a ratio of 2:3. In other words, an important aspect of the composition should be placed about two-thirds of the way across the paper to create a harmonious picture. This can be on the vertical or horizontal lines, so is appropriate for landscape and portrait viewpoints.

Using a viewfinder

To make composing a picture easier, try making a portable viewfinder. Use a fairly thick piece of card, about 4in x 51/2in. Cut a rectangle of 1in x 11/2in from the middle of the sheet. Hold it away from you, shutting one eye, and look at the composition. Use this to "frame" your subject to decide the best viewpoint to begin drawing from.

Using the Golden Mean principle ensures the best composition for your drawings and paintings

Although it takes time to master, perspective will boost the realism of your pictures

The basics of perspective

Perspective in a drawing is what gives it its sense of depth. Imagine the drawing of a long straight road. If you were standing looking directly up it, the lines which mark the edges of the road would seem to converge as they fade away into the distance. The point at which these two lines meet is known as the vanishing point.

Of course, we know that these lines are in fact parallel and do not actually converge at all. However, this optical illusion gives an immediate sense of distance. Artists use this optical trick to give their work a sense of realism. It looks incredibly complicated, but the effect of perspective is fairly easy to achieve and, as with most technical areas of drawing, will become easier the more often you practice it.

The main elements of perspective

The horizon line

This is a horizontal line, which is roughly level with the observer's eyes. If the observer changes position, such as when sitting or standing, so too does the horizon line.

The point of view

This is the direction in which the observer is looking.

The vanishing point

A composition that uses perspective will have at least one vanishing point, which is usually situated on the horizon line. There are three types of vanishing point: parallel perspective, oblique perspective and aerial perspective. These types of perspective are directly related to the number of vanishing points within the composition.

Parallel perspective: this is when all the parallel lines appear to converge to one point in the picture.

Oblique perspective: this is when there are two vanishing points, at different points of view along the horizon line. The horizontal parallel lines recede toward the horizon and form two converging sets of lines, which meet at their respective vanishing points.

Aerial perspective: this is slightly different to either parallel or oblique perspective, as the vanishing point is above or below the horizon line. Often aerial perspective will be used alongside oblique perspective, which gives the subject of a composition a feeling of height or depth.

Parallel perspective – simple exercises

Parallel or "one-point" perspective is the easiest type of perspective to draw, as there is only one vanishing point. Look at how the box in the illustration is drawn so that all the parallel lines converge as they move into the distance.

- Try drawing a similar box several times, altering its width and height.

- Once you feel comfortable doing that, see if you can attempt the room shown in the two remaining illustrations. It is guided by exactly the same rules. Only the parallel lines that recede are affected, while the horizontal and vertical lines, which are parallel to the paper's edges, remain unaffected.

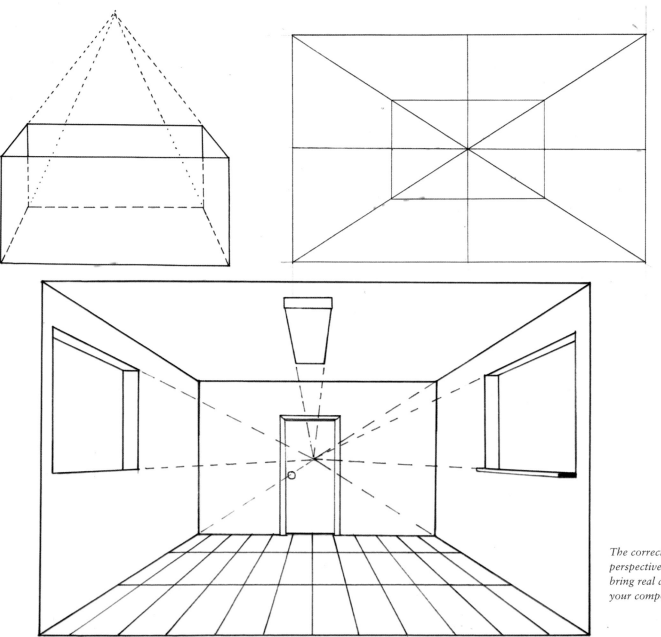

*The correct use of
perspective will
bring real depth to
your composition*

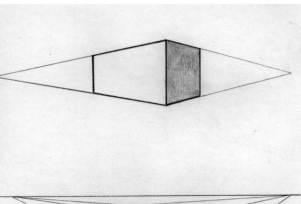

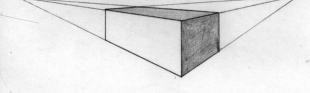

Artists use perspective as a kind of optical trick that helps pull the viewer into the picture

Oblique perspective – simple exercises

If you are using an oblique, or "two-point," perspective you can create compositions which have subjects placed at an angle. This is very useful when drawing buildings, as often they are placed at different angles in relation to each other.

- Use a box similar to that in your first perspective exercise. Place two vanishing points on either side of your horizon line and use them to create your guidelines. The lines should converge at the front edge of the box.

You can even alter the viewpoint of an object using oblique perspective: distant, close-up, "bird's-eye," and "worm's-eye" view. Try the following exercises:

- If the box is viewed from a distance, the box appears smaller with little distortion of the sides, which slope back at less of an angle than a box, which is closer.

- If the vanishing points are close to the subject on a normal horizon line, you will get the effect of an object which is very close to you. This is called "foreshortening." The sides of the box seem quite distorted.

- A low or "worm's-eye" viewpoint means that the horizon line moves down the box. This makes any converging lines of perspective above the horizon line appear steeper.

- A "bird's-eye" viewpoint is created by moving the horizon line upwards, which gives an effect of looking down onto the subject.

- By adding a third or "aerial" vanishing point, you can give a further feeling of height to a composition. This works especially well when drawing tall buildings.

Other ways of giving a sense of perspective

You can also give a sense of perspective within a composition by using tone and colour. These will be discussed in more detail later in the book.

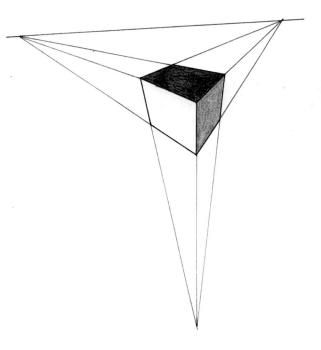

While you should never blame your tools for a job done badly, it is essential to have the right equipment to help create the best end result. Follow this practical guide and you will have the perfect companion to accompany you on your first steps as an artist.

Selecting the Best Tools

Pencils

The most common drawing material is the pencil. Often called a "lead pencil," it is actually made of graphite and comes in many different degrees of hardness. These range from 9H to 8B.

Pencils are incredibly versatile and are the most popular medium to use when drawing and sketching. They are portable and mistakes can easily be erased. They are also very cheap and can make a seemingly endless array of marks. Pencils may seem less glamorous than some of the other drawing materials available, but for sheer versatility and ease of use, the humble pencil cannot be beaten.

- H indicates "hard" when grading pencils. H pencils are best suited for technical drawings, as they are harder to use due to the marks they make. They will indent paper easily and are hard to erase, making mistakes difficult to remove. They are also less fluid that the softer B pencils.

- B indicates "soft," meaning that the marks on the paper are darker, softer and wider than those of a harder H pencil. It is the B selection of pencils that most artists will use when drawing. They are much easier to manipulate and can be erased easily, as well as smudged and blended to make a range of tonal and textural effects.

Always use a good quality pencil as poor examples will give an uneven mark and may damage your drawing surface. There are some excellent tins available which contain the full range of artists' graphite pencils. You can experiment with all the different gradings, replacing individual pencils as you use them up. Some pencils will make different graded effects, according to the brand, so once you find a pencil you like, stick to that manufacturer so you will always know what you are getting.

You may find that at times you will need a harder pencil for very detailed compositions. A good range of pencils will include a 2H pencil for precise drawing; an HB for basic note-taking and quick sketches; a 2B for most sketching tasks, and a 4B and 6B for heavier shading and tonal work.

There are other drawing materials that are considered similar to the common pencil. These include:

- Pure graphite sticks: use as you would a normal pencil. These are sticks of pure graphite, encased in a thin film of plastic, which make wide strokes when used on the angle.

- Sepia sketching pencil: this is a brown pigmented pencil, which was traditionally used when sketching a subject onto a canvas for painting. Used on its own, it produces a pale brown line which is smudgable and water-soluble. It is a type of chalk.

- Sanguine sketching pencil: this gives a richer brown colour and is also used to sketch onto a canvas. It is often used alongside white chalk on coloured paper.

- White sketching pencil: this can be used as a highlighter with pencil, charcoal or chalk, or on its own on coloured paper.

Drawing Equipment and Materials

Coloured pencils

Coloured pencils are similar to graphite pencils. The colour is made by mixing pigment, clay and wax. The softness of the pencil is determined by the amount of wax.

You can create all sorts of effects with coloured pencils, including overlaying different colours, although they cannot be mixed together in the way paint can. This means that there are hundreds of different colour variations available to give you as much choice as possible. Because you do not have to mix the colours yourself, they are a good way of beginning to explore collared compositions.

Some collared pencils are also water-soluble, which gives the added benefit of being able to add water to create an effect like watercolour paints. The pencil colour is applied to the paper as normal, and then water is applied with a brush, which mixes the coloured pigments together as a "wash." This gives a pale, delicate feel to a drawing and can be used throughout the entire composition or as highlights.

Charcoal

One of the first drawing materials ever used were pieces of charred wood from the fires of prehistoric man. This ancient drawing tool is still used today in the form of charcoal. It is made from willow sticks, which are prepared in kilns.

Charcoal is incredibly easy to use and can make loads of different marks and tonal effects. It is not really appropriate for fine detailed work but is excellent for producing free-flowing, expressive compositions.

Charcoal needs to be "fixed" once the drawing is completed to prevent smudging. There are lots of different fixative sprays available for this.

There are many types of charcoal available pencils, compressed sticks and twigs.

- Stick charcoal is made from kiln-fired willow twigs and comes in many grades of thickness. They are the most natural form of charcoal. They are more breakable than the other forms of charcoal available but their delicate structure means that the smaller sticks can produce some quite fine detail.

- Compressed charcoal is easier to use as the charcoal powder is mixed with a binder to make a thicker stick, which is harder to break. Consequently, it is less effective for fine detail but can fill in large areas of tone quickly.

- Charcoal pencils can be used as you would a normal pencil but give the effect of charcoal. They are cleaner to use and can create detailed compositions as they can be sharpened, but they are less spontaneous than charcoal sticks.

- Use white chalk as a highlighter when drawing with charcoal for a dramatic contrast.

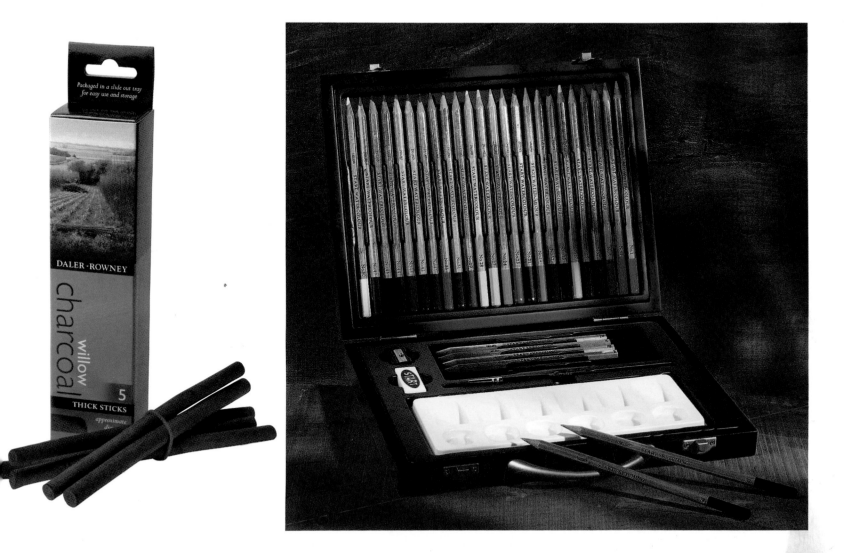

Drawing Equipment and Materials

Pastels and crayons

There are two main types of pastel – hard and soft. They produce quite different effects and can be purchased in many colours. They are made by combining pigment, chalk and gum. Soft pastels have a very particular bloom, which is velvet-like, with rich tones that can be blended together to create very delicate effects. Hard pastels contain more binder and so are less vibrant, although they are easy to handle and can be used to add detail and fine lines to a composition. They can also be purchased in pencil form. Pastels can be rubbed away with a clean rag or a finger. Any finished piece should always be fixed using a spray varnish.

- Oil pastels give an effect similar to oil paint with their rich, thick pigments. They are very moist and give a painterly feel to a composition. They are soft and can be applied light over dark, which is useful as mistakes are hard to remove. The best way is to scrape excess oil pastel away with a sharp craft knife or fingernail, then reapply colour over the top.

- Wax crayons are similar to oil pastels. They are an ancient medium and were common in Egyptian times. They are greasier than oil pastels and if layered, produce an impermeable, smooth finish. It is difficult to use lighter colours over dark wax crayons, so colours need to be carefully planned. If mistakes are made, a sharp knife can scrape away excess wax. This can be used as a technique to allow lighter colours to be highlighted through the darker ones. Wax crayons do not need fixing.

- Conte crayons are very compressed chalks which are harder than pastels. They are available in a range of muted colours and are traditionally used for creating tonal studies. Conte crayons do not need fixing.

Pens and markers

The first basic pens were simply sticks dipped into ink. Then feather quill pens were created which allowed for a more constant, fluid line. Nowadays, there are hundreds of different pens of various thicknesses, colour and permanency. Some should be used with dipping ink or cartridges, whereas others have their own inbuilt supply. They are all capable of creating interesting lines and textures.

- Some pens can be used with water to create a wash, similar to the principle behind watercolour painting. This technique softens lines and blocks in subtle areas of tone. Ink can also be spattered, blobbed, stippled and sponged to great effect. These techniques will be described in more detail throughout the book.

- Marker pens give a variety of lines and colours and can be blended by overlaying darker tones over light. The ink is translucent and can cover a large area of paper quickly, giving any composition a very immediate, fresh feel. The larger nibbed varieties make a range of interesting lines and can fill in blocks of colour with ease. There are a huge number of ink types available in a wide range of colours, which are suitable for use with both pens and brushes.

Drawing Equipment and Materials

Brushes

In Chinese art, there is no definition between the disciplines of drawing and painting. This is because all drawing is done with a brush. Drawing with a brush produces a free-flowing, fluid spontaneity. Any type of ink or paint can be used as a drawing medium, or within a mixed-media composition.

Paper

There is a huge range of drawing paper available, both as individual sheets or in a book form such as a drawing pad or sketchbook. Drawing paper is graded according to its weight (gsm, or grams per meter squared), which determines its thickness, and can be bought in a range of sizes and colours. Some paper is textured to produce certain effects or to suit specific materials, whereas other papers are fairly universal and can be used with most drawing mediums.

Often quite unusual effects can be achieved according to the paper type that is used, so it is worth experimenting with lots of different types of paper.

- Smooth paper is good for pencil sketches and pen and ink, as detailed compositions can be created without the drawing medium "bleeding" into the paper. The lines will appear clean and fine. Cartridge paper is an excellent all-round paper for most types of sketching and sketchbooks are often made from it. Hot-pressed paper is very smooth and gives a hard, unforgiving line whereas cold-pressed paper is a little more textured so lines appear softer. Felt

tip pens are best used with hot-pressed paper or card as they bleed easily.

- Textured paper is essential if you are choosing to work with chalk, charcoal or pastels as these drawing mediums will all benefit from having a rougher surface to "key" into. The powdery nature of these types of drawing medium mean that they require a pitted surface in which the pigment can sit. The different grades of paper texture will produce very different effects. Some are very coarse while others give a softer, richer tone.

- Coloured paper adds an extra dimension, especially to pastel and chalk drawings. The most famous coloured paper is Ingres paper, which comes in every imaginable shade and has a soft, velvety surface, which makes it ideal for delicate work. Cheap sugar paper is also suitable and is a cost-effective sketching paper.

When looking at the "weight" of drawing paper, remember that:

- 150 gsm is a good basic sketching and drawing paper.

- 180 gsm is a heavier paper more suited to charcoal and soft pencil compositions.

- 300 gsm is good for coloured pencil washes, watercolour and pen washes, and mixed media.

Other accessories

- Putty eraser: this is a malleable eraser, which can be used to lift pigment off paper, to remove lines or create highlights. It can actually be shaped by hand into a point to erase very small areas of pigment. Putty erasers tend not to damage paper in the way a harder eraser might.

- Hard eraser: hard erasers are better suited for pencil drawings on smooth paper. They are very effective at removing lines, but take care not to rub too hard as you may damage the paper.

- Paper stump: paper stumps are used to blend pigment together in a more delicate way than a finger could achieve. They are sometimes referred to as torchons and are rolled strips of paper, which can be sharpened and reused.

- Drawing board: this is a piece of board onto which you can clip or tape your paper to ensure it does not slip about when you are working.

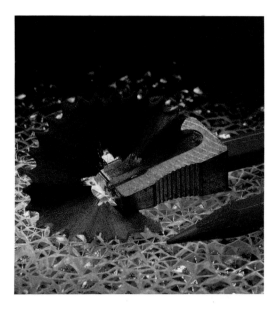

- Fixative: this is a spray varnish which helps to bind the pigment of materials such as chalk or pastel to the drawing surface to prevent it from slipping or smudging.

- Craft knives and sharpeners: these are essential to keep your pencils in top condition, especially when doing fine, detailed drawings. Craft knives are very useful as they sharpen pencils, cut paper, and can be used as a drawing tool in their own right. Use the tip of a craft knife to scratch into paper to lift away pigment for an unusual effect.

Drawing Equipment and Materials

Creating your kit

It is useful to keep all your art materials together to keep them in good condition and easily accessible when something grabs your imagination. An excellent storage solution is to buy a plastic toolbox from a hardware store, as it will have lots of compartments to keep things in, is light, easy to clean, and has a carrying handle.

Another good investment is an art folder, which is a briefcase-style case with a zipper, which will protect your loose papers and can store your precious compositions.

List of basic drawing equipment

This is a list of the very basics. Add to them as you become more confident in experimenting with different materials.

- 2H, HB, 2B, 4B and 6B pencils
- A putty eraser
- A hard eraser
- A small box of water-soluble coloured pencils
- A box of stick charcoal
- A small box of pastels
- Red, blue, and yellow watercolour tubes
- No. 2 and No. 4 watercolour brushes. A larger brush for colour washes
- A fine tipped black fibre pen, a black mapping pen, and a black marker pen
- A small bottle of black ink

- A larger bound sketchbook
- A small spiral-bound sketchpad
- A pad of cartridge paper (150 gsm)
- A pad of cartridge paper (180 gsm)
- A pad of watercolour paper (300 gsm)
- A few sheets of sugar paper in a variety of colours
- A can of fixative
- A craft knife
- Paper tissues for wiping and blending
- Masking tape for securing work onto a drawing board.

You needn't spend a small fortune on putting together the best equipment for achieving your artistic goals

Learn to "See" not "Look"

Most compositions tend to be from direct observation such as still life, portrait or landscape drawing, or painting. As a beginner, you will spend a lot of time observing a wide range of subjects as you plan and create your compositions.

You can find inspiration for your compositions all around you

An artist has to learn to look at the world through new eyes. All those things, which you previously took for granted, must be viewed afresh, in order for you to break a subject down into its various components: form, tone, texture, colour, etc.

- Learn to see rather than simply look. Train your eye to constantly be aware of how things relate to each other to help you plan successful compositions. For example, sit down and look around your room. Begin to break down each item in your eye-line into simple shapes, then observe the way in which those shapes relate to one another – do they overlap? How are they grouped? Where does your eye naturally rest? How could they be made into a pleasing composition? Do the same again, but think about texture, tone, or colour.

- Use a subject in two different ways – accurate observation or subjective starting point. Take an object, person or view and using the exercise above, look at them in a very analytical, objective way, as if you were doing a representational composition. Think about what you see. Then, move away from your subject for a while. When you return, begin imagining how this subject affects you, what it makes you feel. How would you begin to think about representing this subject in a more emotive, subjective way?

- Don't assume that a subject is always the same. Remember that objects, spaces, and subjects can alter according to factors such as time, light, mood, etc.

- Will the subject dictate the medium and/or style of the drawing or painting? Think about the practicalities – if you are quickly sketching skies, or a busy market, then pencil, pens or watercolours will capture the essence of the subject and are portable. A still life could be tackled in pastels or oils with plenty of time for fixing or drying.

What is your objective? Think about what the composition is – a sketch? Research material? A finished composition? Is it objective or subjective? Think about the previous exercises and how you can relate them to your aims for a particular picture. Try to communicate your perception of the subject. Don't be afraid to ask questions, and be enquiring about how the materials you are using will affect technique, structure, and form.

- Keep attempting different subjects. The more you draw and the wider your subject knowledge and understanding, the quicker you will begin to develop your own style and imaginative confidence.

- You can invent your compositions – but you need to have basic technical knowledge and foundation skills to turn imagination into art. Connecting the visual to the technical will allow you greater artistic freedom.

- Develop your hand-to-eye coordination. Remember to allow your own interpretation of the subject to shape your composition and give it warmth and depth.

If you can maintain a certain amount of enthusiasm for the subject, even though you are thinking about the technical aspects of creating a composition, you should be halfway to creating a visually stimulating piece.

There's no need to create a finished masterpiece as soon as you sit down – do your research, make visual notes, and plan that imaginative painting

Using a Sketchbook

Developing your Skills

To become an artist, and to think and feel the way an artist does, requires patience and practice. A few minutes sketching each day will ensure that your brain, eye and hand coordination improves quickly, allowing you to attempt increasingly challenging techniques and compositions.

Many artists spend a lot of time between compositions practicing their techniques, collecting information about subjects which inspire them, collating and developing that information, and experimenting with ideas. The ideal place to gather together all these various elements is within a sketchbook.

- One of the best ways of following your artistic progression is to create a sketchbook which you can practice in every day. Imagine it as an exercise program – 15 minutes each day will keep you in trim artistically.

What is a sketchbook?

A sketchbook is an essential piece of equipment, which should be used as an artistic aid. In it you will do several things: practice, experiment, keep notes and records, and most importantly, build your confidence.

The practical considerations when purchasing a sketchbook are:

- How big is it? There is no point in having a sketchbook which is too big to transport easily. However, it needs to be big enough to hold the information you require comfortably. A good solution is to have two sketchbooks running concurrently – a small one for keeping in a pocket or handbag at all times, and a larger one for home and location studies.

- What is it made of? It should be hardback or spiral-bound cartridge paper, although if you prefer working in a certain medium, such as pen and ink, pastel or watercolour, you may wish to purchase a sketchbook with paper that is more suitable for that technique. General drawing, sketching, and note-taking will still be required at times, no matter what your choice of medium, so you will need a basic sketchbook as well.

How do I use a sketchbook?

Remember that a sketchbook is not a finished composition. Think of it as a personal visual and technical aid. You can develop your confidence without fear of judgement, as you can make as many mistakes as you wish. Make a point of practicing some sketches without an eraser of any kind – this way you will see the mistakes you have made and can refer to them the next time you go to draw that subject.

- **Practice** – use the sketchbook to try new techniques and hone your skills. Everything from small studies of different lines and textures, rules of perspective or attempting sketches of individual subjects can be tried out within its pages.

- **Experiment** – attempt new things regularly, whether it be a different medium or technique. You can even invent your own ways of mixing mediums together to produce unusual effects. Some may not work, but you will learn a lot from trying.

- **Record keeping** – one of the crucial functions of a good sketchbook is to act as a reference point for more finished compositions. Use it to record detail, which will have an influence on the final composition: texture, tone, detail of colour, etc. Look at the subject from different angles and make brief sketches to help you visualize it more clearly when you are finalizing the structure of the picture.

Sketchbook exercises

- Divide a page into four equal boxes. Choose a subject – such as a piece of fruit or a view from your window – and draw it four times over a week. See how your interpretation changes. You should find that the sketches become more fluid.

- Limit yourself to a time, say 30 seconds or two minutes, and then sketch something within that time frame. Do this each day for a week and see how much quicker you get at capturing the essence of a subject.

- Collect postcards, cuttings from magazines, interesting scraps of fabric, and photographs. Paste them into your sketchbook for reference and as a starting point for a composition. Visually stimulating items will help fire your imagination.

- Try limiting yourself to three or four colours. You will learn how to blend more quickly if you have less of a range to choose from.

- Experiment with different ways of making marks in your sketchbook. Use the other end of a pencil or paintbrush, or your fingers, dipped in ink or paint to see what marks you can make. An old comb or toothbrush can be dragged through paint or ink to make interesting textures.

- If a subject has lots of exciting qualities, make several sketches, which focus on each one in turn: form, detail, colour, tone, or texture for example.

- Attempt to create an abstract interpretation from an everyday object.

- These exercises can be repeated over and over again using different subjects, materials, and colours. Try to do at least two a week to keep artistically "fit."

Using a Sketchbook

Using a sketchbook on field trips

One of the most important functions of your sketchbook is to be a portable studio. This means that you can easily capture things of interest while you are out and about. Many artists find a great deal of their inspiration occurs when they are outdoors, among nature and everyday scenes. If you have a sketchbook and pencil handy, you will be able to make quick sketches, which can be developed into a completed picture at a later date.

Sometimes you will make pre-planned trips, at other times a subject will grab you when you least expect it, so keep that sketchbook to hand at all times.

If you are planning a field trip to study a certain subject, you should make some basic preparations to make your trip as worthwhile as possible.

Planning a sketching trip

It is a good idea to be prepared for a sketching field trip. There are a few basic steps that you can take to make sure you do not have a wasted journey.

- Be prepared for changes in the weather – some places may be fine one minute, then pouring with rain the next. However, this doesn't mean that you cannot collect some valuable material – after all, the weather will give an interesting perspective on the subject. Take a raincoat, which can be folded and stored, at the bottom of a waterproof rucksack. Also, take some refreshments and dress appropriately, as you will not be inclined to sit sketching if you are too hot or too cold.

- Choose a sturdy bag, such as a rucksack, for carrying all your materials in as you may want to travel quite far to view certain subjects. A good waterproof bag will last for a long time and will protect your equipment.

- Take a range of sketching materials as you may wish to capture different aspects of a subject, which are better suited to certain types of medium. Remember to take a bottle of water along if you intend to use watercolours or water-soluble pencils.

- Take a craft knife to sharpen pencils and create scratching effects. Also pack an eraser, a soft clean rag, and a selection of brushes plus paper clips to stop your papers from blowing about.

- Some people like to have a small, collapsible stool to sit on. A plastic sheet will make a comfortable, easily transportable and light alternative.

When you are working outdoors, you will not be in control of your subject in the way that you are over a still life. You may find that the scene or subject that you are trying to capture is constantly changing, so you will have to learn to sketch quickly.

- Don't waste time on elements of the subject which can be left out or added later on.

- Make a few notes to support your sketch to help you remember details.

- Focus on the essential information that you need to capture, and choose an approach and the materials that will help you to do this.

- If you are not able to sketch your intended subject for some reason, then try something else – you may be pleasantly surprised by the results.

- Remember, your intended subject may not be as helpful as you would like. Animals have a habit of moving around, as do people, so you may find you have to attempt several sketches at the same time. That way, you can return to each one as the animal shifts to and from a particular position.

Supporting material

You may find that you want to take some photographs or notes to help support your sketches, which will aid you when developing them into a final composition. You can make your initial sketches in pencil or charcoal, then use a photograph to provide information about colour, or a few written notes explaining the quality of the light.

- Use photographs to give you a range of compositional viewpoints.

- A general reminder of the scene or subject is useful when creating a final picture.

- Capture specific elements, such as colour or form, in a photo which can be referred to later.

- Use a photograph as inspiration for starting a composition.

- Certain subjects, such as a bird flying, can be captured on camera more easily than in a sketch, and then used as the basis for a finished piece.

However, do not rely on photographs alone when composing a picture. Copying a photo will result in a dull, lifeless piece of art.

Make location sketch notes to help you remember details about a scene or subject. You can also incorporate these notes into a sketch for additional reference. Simple words or bullet points will enable you to cross-reference several drawings and photographs far more easily.

Field study exercises

- Choose a view that inspires you, and over the course of several visits, sketch it using different mediums and from different viewpoints. When you feel you have really got to know the scene, attempt a composition from memory, drawing on the essence of the subject, as opposed to the technical details.

- When sketching wildlife, limit yourself to a time – say 30 seconds – so you can attempt to create a fluid representation, which contains the very basic elements of the subject. Zoos, nature reserves, and parks are great places to study different types of creatures. Concentrate on the overall posture and proportions rather than detail.

- Choose a subject such as a flower or tree, then sketch it over a period of weeks. You will learn how it changes and alters according to the seasons, weather, and light quality. Decaying plants can produce fantastic shapes and textures.

- Choose a theme, such as trees or buildings, and gather together as much information in the form of sketches, photographs, and magazine clippings. Be on the lookout for any interesting examples when you are on your travels.

- Always take your sketchbook with you when you go on vacation. Different countries have a vast array of wildlife, landscapes, buildings, and people that can provide you with new subjects to tackle. Many of these will inspire you as you view them, so be sure to take plenty of notes to allow you to create a composition when you return home.

- Try sketching a scene at different times of the day. The light quality in the early morning will be entirely different to that at dusk. Watch how the shadows fall and the tonal values change.

Try to complete at least one of these activities each week, even if you choose a view from your window. There is nothing like sketching from life to give your compositions a firm foundation of form and structure. Knowing how something moves grows or changes according to the weather, light, and conditions will enable you as an artist to interpret your chosen subject with far more clarity and feeling.

The following chapters contain exercises that are ideal for practicing in a sketchbook. That way you will have a continuous record of your improvement as an artist.

BASIC SHAPE

Deep yellow

violet

Ultramarine

White

Applying paint

Add detail

Blended

Lines, Texture, and Tone

Follow these simple exercises to begin mastering your pencil work and your experimentation with different types of medium. Remember that practice is very important if you want to start on the road to becoming an accomplished artist.

Exercise 1

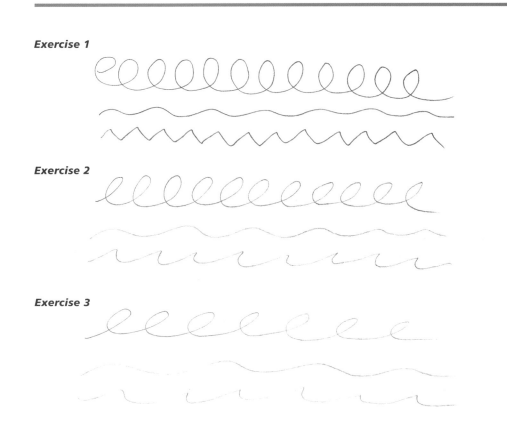

Exercise 2

Exercise 3

LESSON 1

One of the most important things you need to learn before you even make a mark is how to hold your drawing equipment. There are essentially two ways of holding a pencil or other drawing implement. Most people will grip the implement, for example a pencil, near the drawing point, then move their fingers and wrist to produce a tight linear control, as you would when writing. The other way is to hold the pencil more lightly, releasing the tension from the fingers and wrist.

The drawing action should instead come from the shoulder and through the elbow, with the wrist acting as a shock absorber and remaining loose and fluid. The shaft of the pencil can be held further up, depending on the type of mark you wish to make – the higher up your fingers, the more fluid and loose the line. Try to avoid resting your hand or wrist on the paper as you draw.

Exercise 1

Take an HB pencil, holding it as if you were about to write your name, and draw the looped, wavy and zigzag lines indicated. You should find that it feels quite restrictive drawing with a tense hand and wrist.

Exercise 2

Now, using the same pencil, move your fingers up the pencil shaft and repeat the exercises. This time you should find that there is more fluidity in your wrist, and that the action should come from your shoulder.

Exercise 3

Repeat the exercises again, this time holding the pencil shaft even further up. Really move your arm as you draw, allowing the pencil to travel lightly and smoothly across the page. The lines should appear very free and spontaneous. Compare the three exercises and see the difference that simply changing the position of your hand can make.

Exercise 4

Now draw the looped circles with the technique from Exercise 2. Each time concentrate on keeping the line evenly spaced, continuous, and fluid.

Exercise 5

Your hand, wrist and arm should be loose now. Using the HB pencil, make the range of marks shown. Don't worry if you feel that you are making mistakes – simply repeat any marks you are not comfortable with until you are happy. The marks should allow you to experiment with wrist movement and moving your pencil in different ways over the paper. Repeat the exercises with a 2B pencil to see the effects that can be produced by using another grade of pencil.

Exercise 4

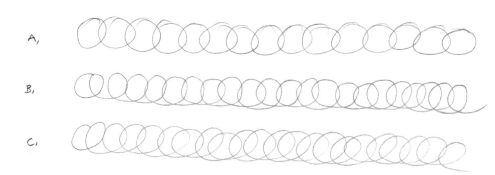

Exercise 5

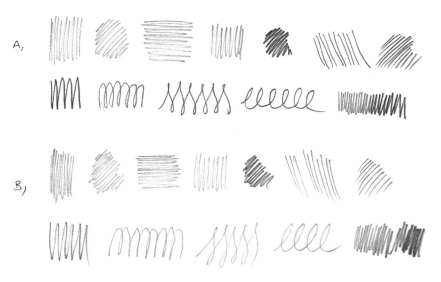

Making Marks

Exercise 6

Exercise 7

Exercise 6
This grid is made with HB, 2B, and 4B pencils, and combines a wide range of strokes: vertical, horizontal, short, long, angular, and curved. Each box contains a mixture of the pencil grades to show how one type of mark can vary according to the materials or pressure used. This is a useful bank of marks, which you can refer to when attempting to create texture in a composition. Copy these or make up some.

Exercise 7
Although it may seem as though there are an indefinite number of lines to be made, in fact there are four basic types. The four boxes are drawn using these lines to show how one object can change according to its linear quality. These lines are:

- **Wire line** – this is a clean, constant line, which is used for sharp, definite outlines.

- **Calligraphic line** – a more uneven line as the width is variable, making it useful for emphasizing tonal qualities.

- **Broken line** – this is a short line which is used repeatedly to convey a more subtle outline.

- **Repeated line** – a free-flowing, fluid type of line which has an organic feel. It is a series of loosely parallel lines, which build up to form an outline.

Draw these boxes, and then attempt a circle or shape to get used to applying the different lines to an object.

Exercise 8
The three techniques shown are examples of methods used by artists to give the feel of three-dimensional tone to an object. Lines are repeatedly criss-crossed either in a regular or

random way. This is known as hatching, for lines going in one direction, or cross-hatching for lines which oppose each other. These strokes may be straight or curved.

You should now feel a little more confident about how to use a graphite pencil and the effects that can be created by simply altering the type of stroke, pressure, and hand position. Keep practicing so you become confident in using these basic marks as they will be the foundation of any composition.

LESSON 2

Now you have grasped the basics of handling a pencil, you can begin to experiment with other types of medium. The following exercises will help you to use a wide range of materials to make interesting marks.

Exercise 1

Use a 6B pencil to make a range of marks. See if you can think up a few of your own. Don't be afraid to experiment – smudge with your fingers, press very hard or as lightly as you can, use the tip or the edge of the pencil, and vary your hand movements.

Exercise 2

Do exactly the same as before, but this time use coloured pencils. Try cross-hatching two or more different colours to see what effects you can achieve.

Exercise 3

These marks are made with wax crayons. Using a craft knife, scratch into the cross-hatching to create interesting marks and effects.

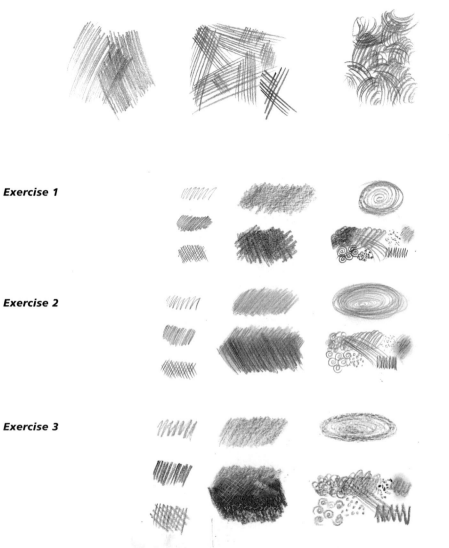

Exercise 8

Exercise 1

Exercise 2

Exercise 3

Exercise 4 – 5

Exercise 4
Use a charcoal stick to make bold expressive marks, which feel quite different to pencil. Get messy – work the charcoal with your fingers to make tonal forms.

Exercise 5
Do the same as you did with the charcoal stick, but this time, use a charcoal pencil to understand the subtle differences between the two similar materials.

Exercise 6
Use some scraps of coloured sugar or Ingres paper to see how certain materials react to a coloured background. The materials shown here are, from left to right: a pastel stick, a white chalk pencil, sanguine oil pencil, carbon stick, and sepia light pencil. Experiment using other mediums to see the range of effects you can produce.

Exercise 7
This example shows how coloured backgrounds affect materials. A range of oil pastels are used to highlight the difference between light and dark backgrounds and how they change the way we see the colour of the applied medium.

Exercise 8
Oil pastels can be overlaid, hatched, scratched, smudged, and applied with degrees of pressure to produce a range of effects and colour combinations. This exercise would also work well with chalk and soft pastels.

Exercise 6

Exercise 7

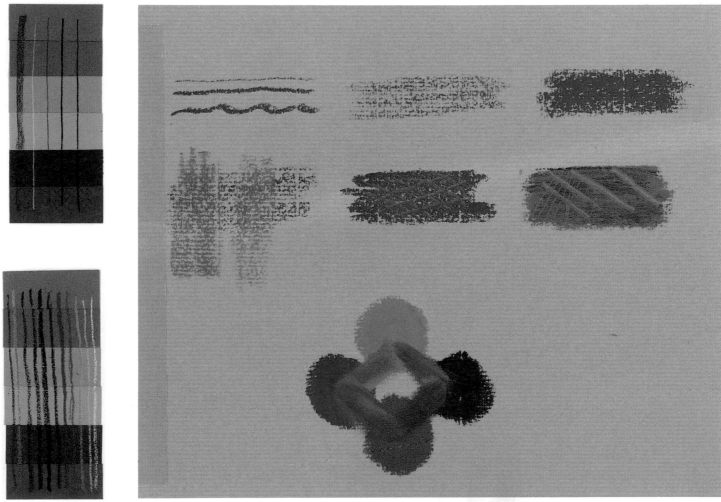

Exercise 8

47

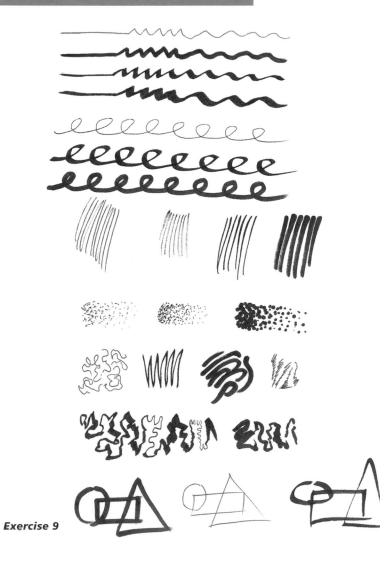

Exercise 9

Exercise 9
Use a range of pens – ballpoint, mapping pens, calligraphy nibs and felt tips or markers – to make a range of marks. See how some pens can give a varied line, while others are more consistent.

Extra exercise
Make your own mark boards, like the two shown. Be very free and expressive. See how the different lines and marks interact with each other.

LESSON 3

You now have the basic techniques to enable you to begin to create pictures. You will be able to use the marks as the building blocks for producing texture and tone within your compositions.

Tone is a measure of light and dark within a painting or drawing and refers to the amount of light which reaches your eyes when you look at a colour. A black and white photograph is made up of tones captured by the camera, so we are able to recognize the images within the photograph even though we do not know what colour they are. When you are applying tone to a composition, think of the subject as if it were a black and white photograph to help you recognize where the dark, mid and light areas of tone are situated.

Exercise 1

Exercise 1

Make a tone scale board. Draw nine squares, then colour the last square black. Now work backwards through to the last square, decreasing the tone as you go. The final square should be almost white. The paper you draw on will represent absolute whiteness.

Exercise 2

Using three of the tones from the tone board, copy the simple landscape. Concentrate on maintaining the three tones consistently throughout the composition.

Exercise 2

49

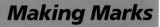

Exercise 3

Exercise 3
Now try using four tones. Copy the simple scene, and then try applying a different range of tones to it. Think about how the light will affect tone – imagine a sunny day and how a dark shadow can affect the tonal quality of a subject.

Exercise 4
Have a go at a very simple tonal still life, like the flowers in a vase shown. Don't worry about too much detail. Instead, think about how to break the picture down into shades of dark and light. Use cross-hatching techniques to give shape and form to your drawing. You can give a feeling of perspective

Exercise 4

by using areas of light and shade to shape objects, giving them a three-dimensional quality.

You should now feel more confident about how to recognize areas of tone and how to apply them in a composition.

Extra exercise
Try the above exercises, this time using colour – pencils, pastels, etc. Remember to restrict the number of colours, and use the darker colours to represent the heavier areas of tone.

The pastel drawing of the South Downs, England on a windy morning is a coloured tonal composition using only five colours to capture the qualities of the mood and light.

LESSON 4

It is now possible to pull all the previous exercises together to start making interesting compositions using a range of marks to indicate line, tone, and texture.

Look at the drawing of the frog. It is a pen drawing, which looks incredibly complicated but is actually made up of three marks – dots, circles, and straight lines – which give the composition depth and texture.

Exercise 1

Take an ordinary household object, such as the cup shown. Draw its basic shape, then use simple hatching techniques to add tone and depth. Now try to draw the same object using dots.

Exercise 2

Continue the theme from Exercise 1, this time adding more detail, texture, and tone to your drawing. Experiment with lots of different types of lines and marks to see how a subject can be interpreted in different ways, according to the method of line you use, such as the three bottles.

Exercise 3

Begin sketching as many different types of texture that you can find. Look at the way texture has been used in the drawing of the squirrel to give the effect of fur and bark. The pen sketch of the fox is much freer, yet is full of vibrant lines. The ballpoint flower sketch relies on texture to give it interest, as the medium is very constant and can appear boring and lifeless. The frog sketch

Exercise 1

Exercise 2

mixes colour and texture to great technical effect, directly contrasting the softer, more fluid feel of the olive tree pencil sketch. Now attempt your own sketches. Look at bricks, trees, plants, animals, fabrics, and anything else around you that is textured. Use your line bank from Lesson 1, Exercise 6, as a guide to the types of mark you can make.

Keep practicing these exercises until you feel really comfortable. You will then be ready to move on to composing beautiful pictures.

The perfect composition, the best textures, the right medium – all can be made redundant without the right use of colour. Study this useful guide to making the very most of your palette.

The Basics of Colour

The colour wheel

A colour wheel will help you to see how the different colours relate to each other, which will assist you when you are mixing colours and applying them to your compositions. The colour wheel is a visual representation of the three main qualities that makes up any colour. These are hue, tonal value, and intensity.

- A hue is simply the name of a colour: red, orange, violet, and burnt sienna are all common examples.

- Tonal value is the darkness or lightness of a colour. A hue can be made darker or shaded by adding black pigment, or lighter or tinted by adding white pigment.

- Intensity refers to how bright or dull a hue is. The stronger the intensity, the more brilliant and vivid the colour. Yellow is a prime example of a strong intensity, whereas violet is weaker, so appears dull.

- This colour wheel is made up of three types of hue: primary, secondary, and tertiary.

Make your own colour wheel and keep it in your sketchbook to help you to understand more about using colour. Draw a circle and divide it into six equal segments.

Primary colours

A primary colour cannot be mixed from any other colour. There are three primary colours – red, yellow, and blue. These colours are very pure and bright, and are very easily recognized. Babies are able to see the difference between primary colours early in their development, whereas other, more subtle hues are difficult to distinguish. Paint the three primary colours onto your colour wheel, positioning yellow at the top, as indicated.

Secondary colours

If you mix yellow and red together, you make orange, which is known as a secondary colour. A secondary colour is always made using two primary colours. Add yellow to blue, making green, then finally mix blue with red to make violet. Add these to your colour wheel as indicated.

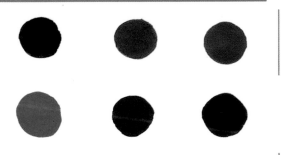

Complementary colours

Red and green are complementary colours. They are directly opposite on the colour wheel and are visually opposed to each other. All primary colours are complemented by a secondary colour, never another primary. Use the colour wheel to learn which colours complement each other. Complementary colours will stand out within a composition, so should be used sparingly so they do not appear too jarring to the eye.

Colours mixed with black

The colours below from the colour wheel have been mixed with black, making the colours shaded. They are duller and darker in appearance.

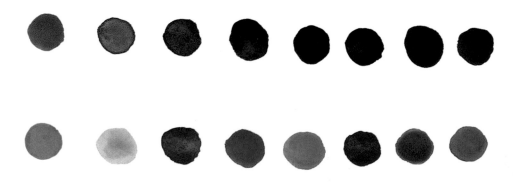

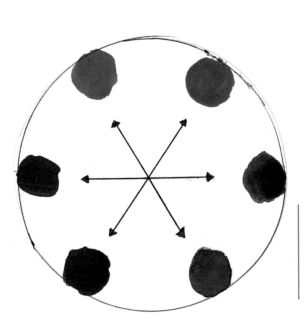

Tertiary colours

Tertiary colours are made by mixing a primary colour with a secondary colour. Red-orange, yellow-green, and blue-violet are all examples of tertiary colours. Position the tertiary colours on the colour wheel between each related primary and secondary colour combination.

Colours mixed with white

The above colours from the colour wheel have been mixed with white, making the colours tinted. They are softer and lighter in appearance.

Colour and mood

Colour is able to convey mood within a composition by initiating an emotive response from the viewer. Look at the two photographs. Both are of a similar subject – still water. Yet the mood in each is quite different because of the colour.

The photograph of the boat is a tonal value composition, with blue as the predominant colour.

It is cool, calm, almost unnerving in its quietness. The colours within give a feeling of emptiness, reflected beautifully in the empty boat, which appears abandoned.

The other photograph is of a sunset, edging into the night. Although the scene is one of solitude, it still appears warm and inviting as the golden yellow tones radiate across the sky and are reflected in the still water.

This shows how important it is to choose the correct colours when creating a composition. Think about the mood you wish to convey, then use the colour wheel to help you select appropriate colours.

Warm and cool colours can change the mood of a painting dramatically – the pears show perfectly how a subject can change depending on the use of colour

Warm/cool colours

If you draw an imaginary line through the colour wheel, down from the yellow to the violet, you can split the two halves into warm and cool colours.

The reds and oranges are known as warm – think of the sun, fire, and a sunset – whereas the greens and blues are cool – flowing water and lush foliage.

It is normal to use a mixture of both warm and cool colours within a composition, although some striking effects can be created by using just a warm or cool palette. The abstract drawings were each made from oil pastel colours from one side of the colour wheel. The pears are also drawn using purely warm or cool colours, to show how a subject can be interpreted in very different ways depending on the colours chosen.

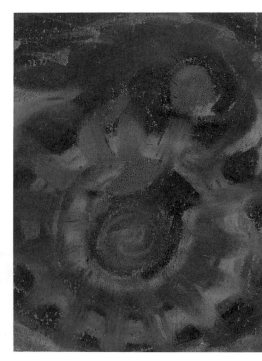

To balance a composition, a mixture of the two palettes should be used. The photographs of the bowl of apples shows how purely tonal colours can make a composition seem cold or lifeless. The predominantly violet and green bowls seem too stark, whereas the yellow bowl is warm and lifelike in appearance.

This is especially true when showing highlights or shadows. If, for example, you are drawing a tree, you can add yellow highlights and blue shadows to show structure and form. Also, you can convey a feeling of depth by adding warm colours to the foreground, while restricting the background to cooler tones.

Using your Palette

Light/dark colours

A drawing can be viewed as light or dark, according to the tonal values of the colours used, just as it could be perceived as warm or cool.

Most drawings contain definite areas of light and dark. Each of these can be rich, warm and forward, or cool and recessive. Adding white or black will respectively lighten or darken a colour, but these tend to have a cooling effect on the colour they are mixed with.

Remember, most white within a composition will be tinted by another hue.

Another way is to add a colour, which is close to the colour you wish to lighten or darken, which will change the hue without cooling it down.

The two pencil landscapes are both drawn with a similar range of colours, although the darker composition contains a far higher ratio of darker hues and tones. It is sombre and oppressive, and the use of the dark paper helps to emphasize this mood. In contrast, the coastal landscape contains much less dark pigment and feels open, bright, and welcoming.

It's the best way to make the move from sketching to progressing your technique – creating a composition based round a still life will increase your confidence while honing your emerging skillset as an artist.

Organizing a Still Life

When you first begin tackling a more complicated composition, as opposed to simple sketches, it is a good idea to begin with a still life.

You may take your time over a still life as you can set it up somewhere without the concern that it will move or change dramatically. This gives you more control over your working conditions.

Do not attempt anything too complicated at first. Instead, set up a simple still life containing two or three basic shapes and colours.

You may position your still life near a natural light source, such as a window, but bear in mind that this will be subject to change. A good alternative is to use an angle-poise lamp, which can be directed at the subject to achieve the exact amount of light and shadow you require.

You will also need to decide whether your composition will be landscape or portrait. Normally, the shape of the subject matter will dictate this – a tall vase of flowers is best done as portrait, whereas a scattered fruit bowl is best captured as landscape.

Decide the approach you wish to take. Is it a subjective composition, such as the colourful oil pastel fruit bowl, which is capturing the essence of the subject? Or a more objective viewpoint that will produce a representational picture, such as the watercolour and pen sketch of the flower vase.

Try to make your composition exciting. Look at the groups of objects. The circles work best when there is a variation in size. The bottle, circle, and box form a more interesting composition when they are not arranged in a straight line and the final example shows how objects should be grouped rather than spread out evenly. Try to use a variety of forms, heights, and sizes to give extra interest.

Drawing rounded shapes

You will discover that many of the objects that you choose to create a still life from will contain circles or curves. It is possible to learn to break down any rounded object into three simple shapes – cylinder, cone, and sphere – then add the detail once you have got the basic form down.

If you look at the top of a glass, plate or bottle from straight on, it will appear flat. When you tilt it slightly toward you, you can then see it is rounded. This flattened circular shape is called an ellipse.

- Practice making simple ellipses by lightly holding your pencil and drawing a flattened circle. Repeat this motion, gradually flattening the circle a little more each time, until you feel confident.

- Drawing a simple circle can seem daunting. Keep your wrist relaxed and draw from your shoulder. You will get better the more you practice.

- Don't press too hard as it makes any mistakes more difficult to erase.

Now attempt the three main shapes: cylinder, cone, and sphere.

- To make the shapes appear three-dimensional, practice varying the depth of the ellipse. You will soon realize when you are over or under-drawing the depth as it will make the shape appear distorted.

- Notice how the glass and bottle are made up from a series of ellipses along a central axis line, in the form of cylinders. Look at some common household objects and break them down into the three separate shapes.

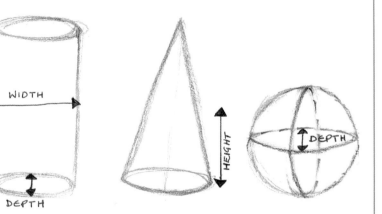

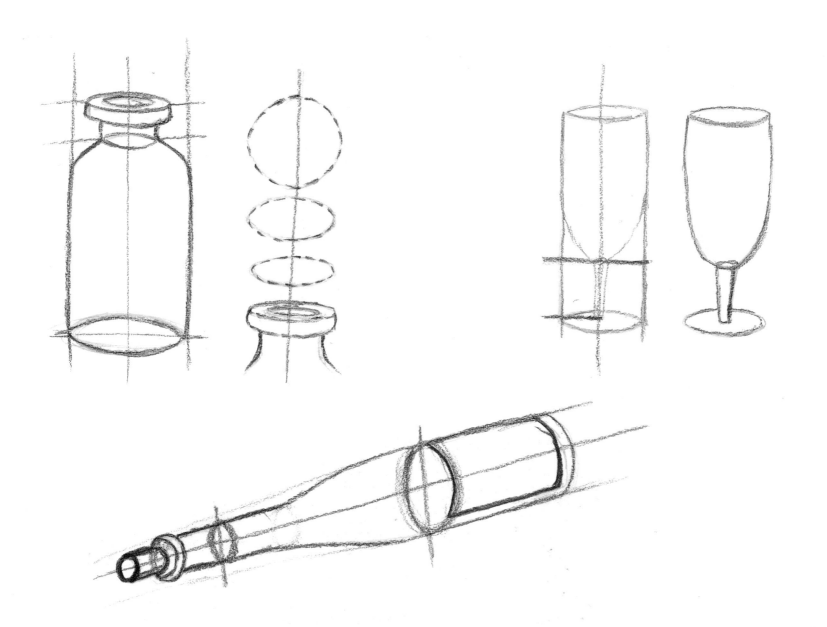

Axis lines

Axis lines will help you to draw realistic rounded objects. They help to position the ellipse at the correct angle. This is especially important if the subject is tilted or at an angle.

- The upright line is the height axis. The horizontal line indicates the depth axis. These lines should always be at right angles to each other.

- Once you have established the height and width axis, you can start to draw in the circle or ellipse. Remember, each quarter mirrors the next.

- Use the horizontal axis to join up two or more ellipses, such as in a bowl or glass. Even if an object is at an angle, the ellipses must still be parallel to one another or the object will appear distorted.

- Try the shapes shown, and then attempt to draw some of your own.

Point of view

These six sketches show how important the compositional element of setting up a still life is. The same group of objects can appear completely different when viewed from different angles.

- The first view is looking down, showing the "bird's-eye" view.

- The second view is looking upwards from a "worm's-eye" perspective.

- The third view is straight on at eye level, with no ellipses showing.

- The fourth view is from the side, with the bowl partly obscuring the lower box.

- The fifth view shows the scene from a more conventional front aspect, looking down into the composition.

- The final viewpoint is from behind, with the two large objects obscuring everything else.

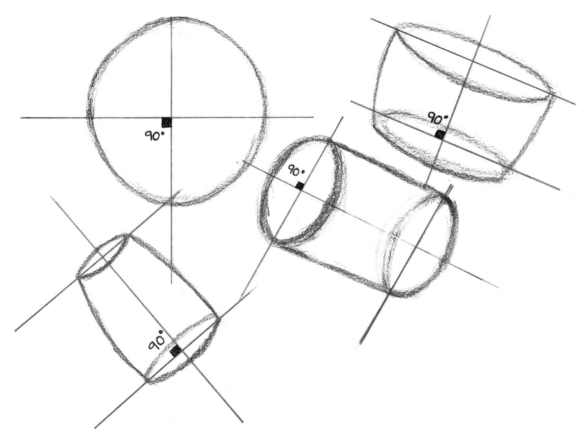

Shadow and light

One of the most important elements of a still life is the lighting and the effects that it creates among the chosen objects. The following examples show how dramatic contrasts can be made by placing the light source in front of the composition, which makes extreme contrasts between light and shadow.

Positioning the light source above the composition creates a quite different effect, which is far more tonal and gives a feeling of solidity. This is a better way of lighting a group of objects as you can see more of the inter-relationship between the various shapes, especially through the intensity of shadow.

Simple shapes

If you look at any still life, you will notice that the composition can be broken down into simple shapes. Continuing on from the sphere, cone, and cylinder, you can now begin to break down more complicated three-dimensional objects.

- Learn to break objects down into simple shapes. They will be much easier to draw. Add detail once you have captured the basic shape.

- Press lightly when sketching in shapes so any guidelines can easily be erased.

- Remember to always draw a central axis, then arrange the ellipses along it. This applies even if the object is at an angle.

- An ellipse at eye level is shallower than one positioned above or below eye level.

- Just because you cannot see part of an object doesn't mean it is not there. Bear this in mind when you position objects close together in a composition. This will ensure the depth of the composition is not distorted.

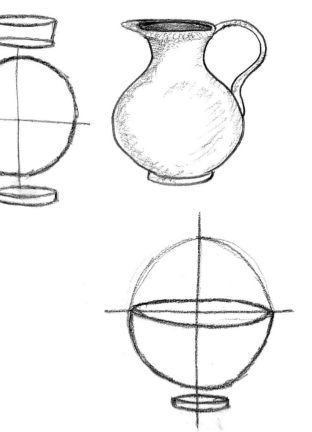

Still life example 1
This simple still life drawing is quite traditional, comprising of a wine bottle with fruit. The composition is very simple and can be broken into simple shapes. It is sketched in pencil, then coloured in with water-soluble coloured pencils.

- **Step one** – the basic shape is sketched out in pencil, leaving the very pale areas white. The darker, shadowed areas are lightly picked out with slight shading.

- **Step two** – basic areas of colour begin to be added, and the guidelines are lightened or erased.

- **Step three** – more colour is added and blended directly on the page, using cross-hatching, smudging, and varying the pressure of the applied colour to create a translucent effect.

- **Step four** – the final details are added, including highlights in the shiny-skinned fruit and the reflective surface of the glass bottle.

Still Life

Still life example 2

Many people think that all still life has to be about flowers and fruit. This composition proves that an exciting painting can be produced from a wide variety of subject matter. In this case, the subject is a dog skull.

The composition is very fluid and relaxed, as opposed to formal or stuffy. The brush strokes are vibrant, and while the subject is observational, the use of texture and light is more subjective. The drawing is focusing on the skull, giving a sketchy feel to the surrounding objects.

Remember, some of the best compositions are successful because they are not over-worked. Do not feel that you have to capture every detail. Instead, learn to give the composition space, and focus on the necessary elements, which convey meaning and emotion.

- **Step one** – the objects within the still life are broken down into basic, simple shapes with a 2B pencil. The lines can be erased as the finer, more detailed sketch is completed. Keeping the shapes very simple to begin with means that the positional aspects can be changed without having to erase detailed drawings.

- **Step two** – next, basic tonal elements of light and shade are added with a 4B pencil. The shadows are smudged to give a smooth appearance, echoing the texture of the skull.

• **Step three** – finally, more detail is added to the
drawing, including a few darker areas picked out
with a 6B pencil to add depth and definition.
Much of the outer area is left unworked which
allows the skull to remain the main focus of the
picture. Highlights are created by lifting away
pigment using a putty eraser.

Landscape

Organizing a Landscape

It is important to approach a landscape with a certain amount of organization. Although creativity is important, there are several structural elements that should be considered before getting down to the composition.

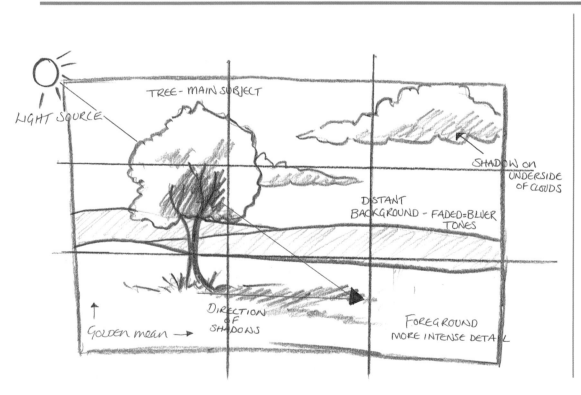

LIGHT SOURCE

TREE - MAIN SUBJECT

SHADOW on UNDERSIDE OF CLOUDS

DISTANT BACKGROUND - FADED=BLUER TONES

DIRECTION OF SHADOWS

Golden mean →

FOREGROUND MORE INTENSE DETAIL

This is especially true if you are on location, as you will have to factor in environmental influences such as weather and light.

- Make a note of where your light source is. In most cases, this will be the sun, or possibly moonlight or a streetlight if you are working at night. In the field sketch of the tree and hills, you can see the position of the sun, and from that work out where the highlights and shadows will form. Should the light change, you will have a basic reference point.

- Use the Golden Mean principle to divide your composition up. This will ensure that the main subject – in this case the tree – is not positioned too centrally which will detract from the rest of the picture.

- Make a few notes in your sketchbook to help you remember important details that you may need, to ensure consistency throughout the composition.

However, don't be afraid to experiment as sometimes the more a composition breaks the rules, the more effective it is.

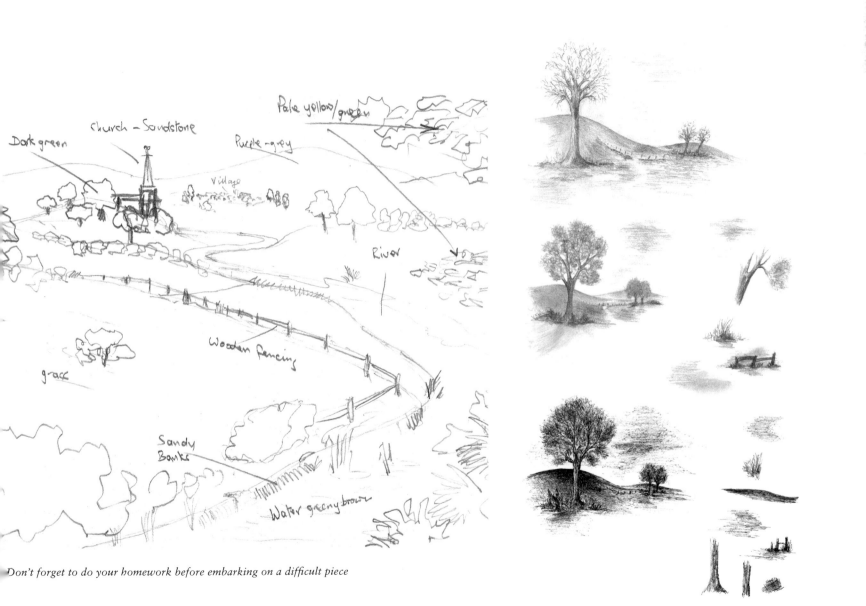

Don't forget to do your homework before embarking on a difficult piece

Landscape

Skies and backgrounds

Skies and background details are crucial elements in any landscape composition – in fact, many artists base their work around particular subjects such as water, sunsets or mountains.

The sunset uses coloured pencils to create a dramatic skyscape filled with rich colour.

In contrast, the watercolour pencil sketch of a boat is delicate, yet fluid. Everything is simple and representational, yet very effective.

The dramatic, almost abstract mountain scene was created by smudging chalk pastels to suggest the idea of blustery wind.

• Have a go at creating a variety of skies and water effects. Try to be spontaneous – often the best effects are those which you least expect. A natural looking sky or water scene should not be overworked. Use the following examples to help you.

Skyscapes

• Use wet-in-wet washes of ink or watercolour pencil to create a cloudy effect.

• Apply small touches of colour to a predominantly white sky to pick out gaps within the clouds.

• Charcoal can be scumbled and smudged to create a tumultuous stormy sky.

Water effects

- Reflections can be picked out using dashes, leaving the white paper to act as the reflected light on the tips of the waves.

- Pencils, pastels or charcoal can be scumbled, dragged, and splattered to create waves and spray.

Trees and flowers

Most landscapes will contain some foliage; even industrial areas contain plant life.

Texture is vital when drawing trees and flowers, as it helps to convey the movement of the leaves, the rough bark or delicate flowerheads.

The photograph of the trees shows the dramatic architectural shapes formed by the skeletal branches.

The leaf shapes are not particularly observational, yet possess a quality of natural light and movement.

The sketches of the violets show how much detail can be achieved using simple pencil marks, then enhanced further by adding colour.

The blackberry twig is a fluid pen sketch, which is a useful reference. The coloured pencil tree is an excellent example of a detailed sketchbook observation.

• Use your sketchbook to collect and practice lots of different types of plant life. Make simple observational sketches that will act as reference material for the future.

The key to drawing trees and flowers successfully is texture

foreground
overpowering

Subject in center of frame
too "square"

Poor Composition

Buildings

Buildings can be quite daunting things for the beginner to tackle, as they are technically more complicated than a more natural subject. The trick is to include the important aspects, leaving out any unnecessary elements, which give a sense of the building without getting overtaken by technicalities. The following examples are different interpretations of how to convey the linear qualities of different types of building, while remaining fluid and interesting.

- The two thatched cottage compositions show the need for careful consideration of where to place the central subject within the wider framework.

- The sketch of a street in Prague conveys the sense of perspective well as your eye travels up the street. There is little detail, but the buildings seem to bustle with interesting architectural elements.

- The drawing of the church gives an even greater indication of the importance of perspective. It reaches upwards, which highlights its significance as an emotionally powerful structure.

- Finally, other elements that require a very linear approach can also be interpreted in interesting and vivacious ways, such as the sketch of a fence post.

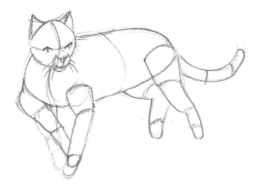

Animals

Many people choose animal sketching as main subjects for their art, as there are so many incredible creatures out there. Animals can be hard to capture, either because they move about too much, or due to the complicated anatomical elements. You can break animals into shapes, as shown in the sketches of the dog, cat, and horse.

Use still images to practice proportions, but always try to see your subject in its natural environment where possible, as this will give you a far greater indication of how it moves and behaves.

Quick sketches may not be as anatomically correct, but will capture the spirit of the subject more comprehensively.

• The linear cat jumping has little detail, yet captures the movement of the leap.

- The sketch of the terrier conveys the charming nature of the subject.

- The sketch of a horse concentrates on the subject's expressive fluidity of movement.

- The tiger sketch concentrates on observing the texture and markings for a future composition.

Make simple sketches in your sketchbook to act as reference material. Always try to convey the essence and spirit of the creature.

Landscape

Landscape example 1

This simple coloured pencil seascape relies on cross-hatching the colours to blend them together.

It is a very basic composition, with the emphasis on colour to convey a feeling of space and warmth.

A basic palette of colours is used: dark and light blue, green, red, yellow, orange, purple, and white.

- **Step one** – sketch out the very basic lines and block in the first colours of the sky, sea, and sand.

- **Step two** – now use a cross-hatching technique to overlap colours to build up the intensity within the composition. Work each layer in the opposite direction from the previous one to allow a certain amount of colour to show through. Add the detail of the boat and grasses.

- **Step three** – use a white pencil to soften the entire composition by cross-hatching over the colour layers. Pick out shadows and highlights on the boat and grasses, using complementary colours.

Landscape example 2

This landscape is drawn with charcoal, and highlights are added with chalk. It is a simple, stylized composition that is subjective in nature. Everything is exaggerated, from the foliage of the trees, through the depth of shadows, up to the brooding storm clouds.

- **Step one** – sketch in the basic outline of the drawing. Block in the darkest areas and draw in the tree trunks and branches.

- **Step two** – begin to add more tonal areas, with the foreground containing the strongest tones which fade towards the background to give a feeling of depth. Add the foliage to the trees in a circular motion and smudge to soften the lines. Repeat this technique to build up the storm clouds.

- **Step three** – finally, pick out more detail with the tip of the charcoal. Add light tones to the tree and clouds by smudging in a little white chalk.

Landscape example 3

This sketch was done on location using a mapping pen. It concentrates on capturing the mood and feel of the subject. The mountains were quite brooding and foreboding, but they were softened by the softer, more textural qualities of the various grasses and foliage.

- **Step one** – a few preliminary sketches were made to decide what types of mark were most appropriate to convey the wide array of textures within the composition.

- **Step two** – a basic linear sketch was put down, keeping the pen lines fluid and light, as any mistakes could not be removed. The darker areas of tone were sketched in.

- **Step three** – the foreground detail was added, with emphasis on maintaining a feeling of space and natural grandeur, without relying too heavily on individual, highly detailed areas.

Landscape example 4

This townscape is an interesting composition as it relies on the mix of rough pencil and mapping pen lines to convey a feeling of energy and movement to capture the hustle and bustle of a busy street.

- **Step one** – sketch in the linear sketch with an HB pencil. The lines are representational as opposed to observational. You should be sketching in very basic shapes to represent figures and objects.

- **Step two** – now begin to add more detail and tone with a 4B pencil. Again, ensure that you keep all your lines very fluid and sketchy. If you make a mistake, don't worry, as it will not detract from the overall composition.

- **Step three** – finally, use a medium-nibbed pen to sketch in details and the main outlines to lift the composition. Keep your wrist very relaxed and draw quickly and smoothly to maintain a feeling of movement and energy.

The human figure is one of the most commonly featured subjects in art throughout history, as it is constantly changing according to the pose or gesture of the subject. It is also notoriously difficult to accomplish.

Proportions of Figures

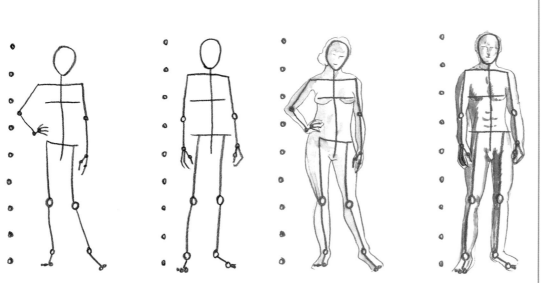

There are some guidelines that make it a little easier to attempt to create a realistic, proportionately accurate figure. Look at the matchstick figures of the man and woman, then at the fully drawn figures. These figures have been drawn using a method which dates back to the Renaissance period, and which is still the most commonly used method of judging proportion today.

- Although no two figures are the same, it is helpful to have a basic guide from which you can judge the correct proportion.

- The most common method was first used by Renaissance artists.

- To judge a figure's proportion, use the head as a unit of measurement. The average male is usually about eight heads tall.

- The distance from the chin to the crotch – the torso – is normally three heads tall. The torso can be divided into equal thirds at the navel and nipples.

- The distance from the upper leg to the knee is two heads tall, as is the lower leg.

- The distance between the shoulders is roughly two heads wide.

- The elbows are roughly three heads length from the top of the head.

- The wrists should be roughly parallel with the crotch, although this will change according to the stance of the figure.

The female figure is slightly smaller than the male, and has two wide points – the shoulders and hips – both of which measure around two heads width.

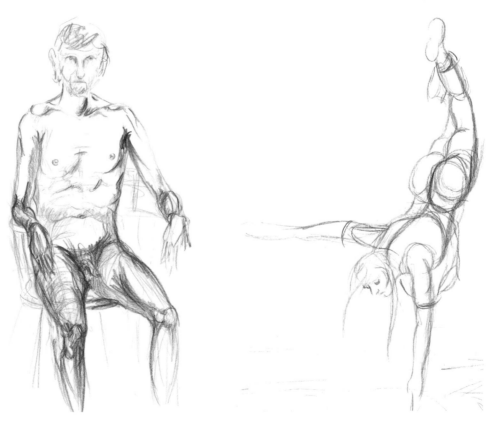

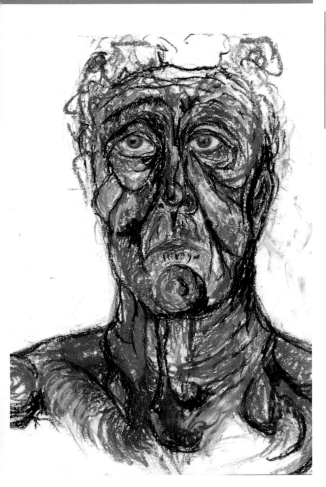

Portrait

Proportions of the head

Drawing the human head is one of the hardest things for an artist to master, and it will take years of practice to become truly competent. However, there is no reason why you should not begin to think about how to structure a portrait.

It is easier to think of the head as an egg on a cylinder. This egg can then be divided up into

rough proportions, which give a basic, stylized version of a human head and features. It is crucial to remember that every face is different, so you will have to develop the ability to turn generic proportions into something that is lifelike and vibrant through practice and experimentation.

- Look at the two structured heads. They are divided up proportionally by the rule of halves. In your sketchbook, draw an egg shape like the ones shown.

- Divide the egg horizontally in half. This marks where the eyes should be positioned.

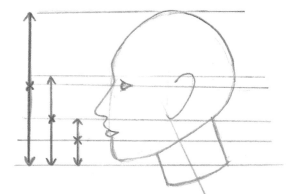

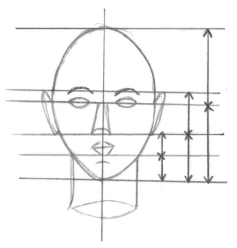

- Position a second line slightly above the eye line to mark where the eyebrows would go.

- Using this eyebrow line, divide the area below in half horizontally. This halfway point is where the base of the nose would be positioned.

- Divide the area below the nose line in half to give the position of the lower lip.

- You should now be able to sketch in the basic features of the human head in their correct positions.

This face is neither male nor female, young nor old. Normally, a woman's features are softer and less defined than a man's. In older people, the features become more pronounced, whereas children tend to have small noses and mouths but comparably large eyes.

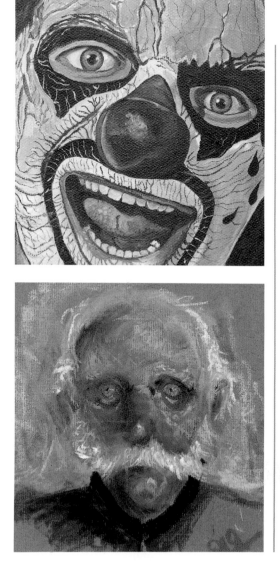

There's no need to be literal when drawing a portrait as the compositions here show – it's more important to capture the character of the subject

Portrait

Portrait detail

The best way to become more confident when drawing figures is to make lots of quick sketches of different parts of the body doing different things. Always try and draw from real life, whether you get someone to pose for you, or just sit in a crowded place and make quick sketches of the people who pass you.

Also remember that the human body is affected by the way the person sits or stands, so you may find that the rules of proportion alter slightly. This is particularly true when you draw a figure close up as, just as with a still life or landscape, the human body is affected by the laws of perspective. This means that the parts of the figure closest to you will seem proportionally larger.

To begin with, keep to sketching figures and portraits from the front, back or side, to get you used to the technique without having to deal with anything overcomplicated.

Above all, keep practicing as much as possible. Before long, you will feel ready to attempt more complex poses.

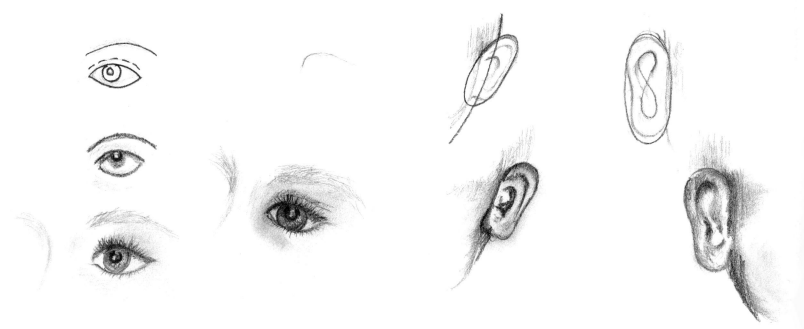

The step-by-step examples on these pages will help you to attempt the harder aspects of portrait and figure drawing, such as eyes, noses, mouths, hands, and feet. Always break the subject up into simple shapes, then add the detail once you are happy with the proportion and positioning.

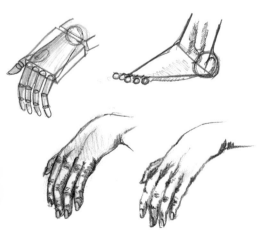

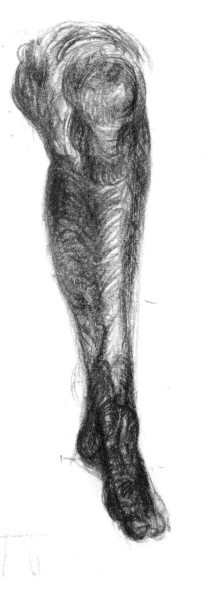

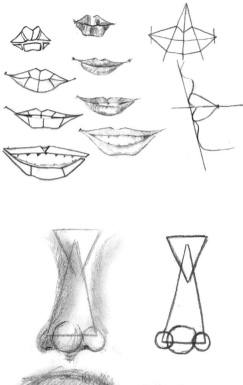

Portrait example 1

These three simple drawings show how you can convey movement by manipulating a simple framework, then "flesh out" the figure around it.

- **Step one** – remembering the rules of proportion, sketch out a framework to help you manipulate a basic figure into interesting poses.

- **Step two** – next, sketch the outline of the figures around the framework.

- **Step three** – finally, add the details that will give your figures a feeling of character and purpose.

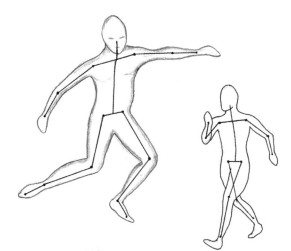

Portrait example 2

This simple charcoal drawing is of an Indian girl. It shows that charcoal can be used to produce a delicate tonal study, which is expressive and observational.

- **Step one** – first, sketch out the face using the rules of proportion, keeping the lines light so mistakes can easily be rectified.

- **Step two** – begin to add in the main areas of shadow, and smudge to soften the lines so as to give a skin-like appearance. Darken the eyes, nostrils and lips.

- **Step three** – lift out pigment to highlight areas using a putty eraser. Define the hair and features with the tip of the charcoal stick and darken the deepest shadows.

95

Portrait example 3

This drawing is done with oil pastels, and is a step forward from the framework figures. It is of a dancing nude, and is more subjective and stylized, allowing the expressive nature of the movement to become the focal point of the picture.

- **Step one** – sketch out the basic figure, using yellow ochre, medium yellow, and violet.

- **Step two** – begin to build up tonal areas of light and dark colour, gently smudging the edges to blend the areas of colour together. Use flesh tones, yellows, and cobalt blue to add definition to the figure.

- **Step three** – warm the composition up with a few lowlights of rich brown, and smudge in a little white as highlights.

Portrait example 4

This is a more traditional formal portrait of a young woman, drawn with collared pencils and a graphite stick.

- **Step one** – draw in the main contours of the face and define the features with the graphite stick. Add a little detail, such as eyebrows, lip tone, and hair texture.

- **Step two** – begin to add colour by lightly cross-hatching the face, overlapping colours to blend new tones. Keep the strokes very light, adding more layers to increase the intensity. This will give the skin a youthful bloom.

- **Step three** – finally, finish by lightly applying a layer of white pencil over the skin to lighten and soften it. Redefine the features and darken any shadows that need more contrast. Pick out highlights in the eyes and hair. Darken the background to allow the face to stand out.

Learn to Paint

An introduction to Painting

A Guide through the Basics

Learning to paint is exciting, creative and above all great fun. It opens up new possibilities in discovering the world that surrounds you. Painting will teach you to become more observant and help you to express yourself through the medium of colour and composition.

Everyone at some point in their life has sat down and painted a picture. More often than not this would have been as a child, for when we are at school we are given the opportunity to express ourselves through art. Sadly though, for a lot of people this activity is lost or forgotten once formal education is over. For others, art never leaves them, whilst some re-discover their enthusiasm for painting later on in life.

This book will help any budding artist to become more informed and experienced, as painting is an ongoing process of learning and discovery. The easy-to-follow exercises will teach you the skills required to compose and paint pictures of your own choosing. The basic rules of composition and perspective will be demonstrated and diverse subjects such as landscapes and portraits will be explored.

The key factor in the process of painting is to master the basic techniques with different painting mediums. These will be shown in the book using watercolour, acrylics and oil paints. There will be guidance on how to utilize colour with the different mediums.

The importance of how to use a sketchbook to record ideas for pictures and the practical use as a learning tool will also be illustrated. Throughout the book the exercises will help you to build up the skills and confidence, to allow you to start creating beautiful pictures with your own unique style. There will be lots of tips on mastering simple techniques, which with practice will give you an excellent basis for producing your paintings. Above all, painting is about having fun with art and using the skills you have learnt from this book.

- The content in this section will provide you with examples of step-by-step methods and techniques which will help you to achieve the necessary skills to develop confidence and technical ability.

- Learn about the usefulness of practicing techniques in a sketchbook and gathering reference material to start creating unique compositions.

- Find out how to utilize different painting mediums to produce an array of textures and tones, which will add perspective and atmospheric qualities to any painting.

- When creating a composition, learn the importance of careful planning with a simple check list.

- Create the illusion of a three dimensional space within a painting by mastering perspective and accurate proportion.

- Discover the different range of painting materials and art equipment available and how to choose the best for your needs.

Use this expert guide to become a skilled painter, but this need not be as daunting a task as you might think.

Understanding the Painting Process

The processes of learning to paint may seem a daunting prospect as there are so many different areas to think about, from understanding colour to which type of paint to use, but everyone has the potential to be able to paint. Children are classic examples of this. They will make marks on paper without any hesitation and express themselves and their surroundings long before they can write.

Throughout history, painting has been one of the most fundamental activities that human beings have done. To record the hunt as in the prehistoric cave paintings, through to the ancient civilisations of the Egyptians and the Greeks. Right up to the present day, painting has been an integral and important form of communication throughout our many periods of history.

A lot of the past that we know about is based on the images painted by artists through the centuries. Many painters have documented the times that they live in and the events in their history, as well as the important subjects, such as their kings and queens. From the formal portraits and countless battles, to simple scenes of everyday life as in the paintings of Van Gogh, painting is part of our lives and history. A painting can often reveal a huge amount of information about the subject, depending of course on how the artist has interpreted the scene or sitter. Painting can make bold statements and has been seen at times to be politically subversive, as in the Surrealists and Cubists movements. Sometimes paintings can cause an up-roar and at other times reduce one to tears, with the sheer beauty of the image in front of the viewer. Throughout history painting has had the power to create emotional responses and you can be part of that process and part of that history.

Paintings have many uses, from portraits to document a person or decorative images to brighten up a dull wall. They can be made in limitless ways and the only restriction is the artist's own imagination.

Painting can convey some kind of message or emotion, such as with a few simple marks on any surface in an abstract form or even as a complex technical piece, creating an expressive statement.

Many people find painting pictures a challenge because they feel that they have to produce a life like representation of the subject they are looking at. In some cases, they create their own pressure by believing that they have to produce that 'masterpiece' with as much detail in as possible. Most often, a good painting is about what you leave out rather than what you put in, so the work on the painting can be minimal and yet still convey some kind of message or emotion. A good artist over time will learn what to leave out of a painting and what to put in, often by trial and error, to create a visually stimulating piece of work. As there are no strict rules in painting, there is nothing to prevent an artist from rendering a scene in any way that they feel will benefit the overall composition. This book will assist you in interpreting any subject in a fresh and spontaneous method which will give emotion and purpose to your paintings.

A painting should be comprised of a series of marks that bring feeling and often meaning. A good painting will work on that level, as opposed to a composition that lacks depth and has little understanding of the overall subject.

A painting of a subject is basically an interpretation as the artist views it. However, the 'super-realists', sometimes known as photo-realists, produce their paintings in a very realistic way which often leaves little room for interpretation. These paintings have merit in the sheer technical ability and keen observation, but do not convey much emotion. Every artist will, with practice begin to develop an individual style of their own.

Before you begin there are certain criteria to consider. If you decide to create an objective painting, you will be looking to produce a realistic or 'lifelike' representation in your composition. This will give an accurate and factual look to the picture and many illustrators use this method to create works of art. A subjective painting will be far more expressive and have passion and emotion, which at times may result in a very abstract composition. Many good artists manage to find a balance between the two styles of painting. There will be occasions when an objective approach is the desired option, especially when it is to record a detail of a time and place, or as a reference in a sketchbook when planning a painting. However, this does not mean that an objective painting should not have any hint of expression, as even these types of compositions should still have life and feeling within them to be engaging.

Sometimes a free-flowing painting could rely on some form of objective elements within it, to make the overall work easily interpreted.

Another consideration for the artist is what type of materials to use for each style of painting.

The effect that you wish to create will be determined by what the painting material will let you produce. For instance, watercolour will give you thin washes of colour which can be blended together, where as oil can give you a thick, bold impasto texture which watercolour cannot give. Acrylic paints on the other hand are designed to give you both styles, but the issue to overcome with this paint is the fast drying time. With practice this is not really an issue and should not put any artist off from using such a great medium. Through trial and error, you will discover which paints work best for your needs and styles of painting you wish to achieve. By the end of this book, you will have a clear understanding of how the various paints perform and what is available to you. You will also have knowledge on the best methods of use that you can apply to the various mediums, for use on your paintings.

The most important aspect of any painting is the use of colour, even if you decide to produce a painting with a limited palette of only a few colours. The effect that different paints can give you would be a matter of experimenting with the mediums to discover what you can achieve with them and the book will demonstrate some of these. You will be guided through the basic rules of using contrasting or complimentary colours within your compositions to create interesting effects.

If you feel inspired by a subject such as a beautiful flower or a stunning view, then you are halfway to creating a successful painting. Most of your paintings will work if you connect with the subject and really start to understand what you are looking at. It is worth trying out the same subject in different mediums and other styles to prevent your work from becoming predictable or stale. Think 'out of the box' and try a change from time to time which should give you a fresh perspective on your favourite subject. Trying new things can

be daunting if you let them and working within your comfort zone is easy, but challenging yourself as an artist is exciting. You may discover that you have talents you never thought possible. There is no right or wrong way to paint, there are no rules and no one to tell you that you can't do that, there are only techniques and methods of application. It is up to the individual artist to experiment and gain more knowledge of the materials and subject matter, which in time will give more confidence to creating stunning works of art. No one artist starts out brilliant at painting, it comes with practice.

From the simplicity of wet paint applied to a surface material, come masterpieces that can have an incredibly emotional impact on the viewer.

Planning your Picture

Before embarking on a painting, you should have a mental checklist of the criteria required for producing a piece of art. If carefully planned, a painting is more likely to work successfully. The result will be more satisfying and rewarding in the end. You will need to consider a range of factors that will influence the final outcome including subject matter, timescale and materials.

Consider these points when planning a painting:

- What expression or emotion do you want your painting to say? How much visual impact do you want your image to have and how will you achieve this? Which style of painting do you want, objective or subjective? If your painting is for research purposes then an objective viewpoint is best. If you want to depict emotion or paint the feel of a specific place, object or particular event, then be more subjective.

- Which of the mediums available will give you the effect you want? Will the painting be produced on location and what level of detail will it contain? Some paints are better suited for detail work than others such as oils or acrylics, whereas watercolour being more fluid is best suited for free-flowing, expressive pictures. All of these mediums will be described in more detail later in the 'materials and equipment' section in the book.

- How much research have you done and is it sufficient? Will you be working from photographs or memory, or are you going to work on location? Will you be using a sketchbook to record all the relevant

information? You may need to make notes or produce several sketches from various viewpoints. Perhaps you could do a series of sketches, some subjective to capture a mood or feeling, or more objective studies to ensure you have all the relevant information required for your paintings. You will learn how to use a sketchbook later in this book.

- How will you apply the image to the paper? Are you working in a 'landscape' or 'portrait' format? What viewpoint will you approach? All of these questions will be tackled in the next section of the book.

The more experience you have, the more confident you will become and these sort of considerations will become second nature to you. If you make some mistakes along the way or forget to include certain aspects, don't worry it won't be a disaster. In fact, you can learn from your mistakes and may even achieve some fantastic results from experimenting.

Creating compositions
What is a good composition? Why is one painting better composed than another? Often it's just because the image feels right or is pleasing to the artist and of course this is still in the 'eye of the

beholder'. As you become more experience at composition, you will remember those elements that can really improve and enhance a painting. Composition is the design and layout within the space of the painting. It should be influenced by the elements that are included in the image or what you want your picture to say. This can include mood, atmosphere, impact, as well as the actual subject matter.

If an image is well composed, it will guide the viewer's eye around the elements of the picture to the main areas or subject matter important to the

design. Perspective is a good example of this when used well in a composition. It will draw your eye in to a painting and so you are directed by the image which is what you want to achieve in a good composition.

An important factor within a composition is the use of space. Every object and space within the design, have a direct relation to each other. These are called the positive and negative spaces, the positive being the subject and the negative being the space around and between the subject. For example, in a landscape the positive space would

be the subjects such as trees, hills, buildings and so on. The negative space would be the areas around and between the objects.

If these elements are interwoven together successfully then the composition and the overall image will work well and be successful. Applying contrasts within a composition will also enhance it. For example, to show how dominant something is, position a small object next to it. Other examples of this are, place light next to dark, thick next to thin, shadow next to light, these contrasts will enliven and improve any composition.

Plan and Prepare

Balance in a composition is important as you don't want the picture to appear much heavier on one side than the other. If you draw attention to one side only, this will affect the basic rhythm of the picture and it will then look unbalanced. Try to keep the eye interested enough to explore the whole picture, without it becoming distracted.

- Add an element within the whole composition to act as the main focal point of interest. This will be that part of the painting where the eye is finally drawn to. This element will usually have some significance to reflect the whole meaning of the painting, perhaps it is the main object or person. Try not to place it too centrally in the design as the eye will naturally go direct to that point. Alternatively, try to lead the eye around the painting by making the composition as interesting as you can.

- Placing objects in rows could make your picture to appear boring and lifeless with no real interesting features to keep the eye stimulated, so this is best avoided. By varying the viewpoint you will create more movement around the picture and also gain a greater depth in the image.

The Golden Mean

The majority of drawings and paintings are produced on rectangular paper or canvas. Most landscape compositions, including seascapes and townscapes, are created with the longer edge of the rectangle as the horizontal line. However, in portrait compositions, the longer edge of the rectangle is used as the vertical, as this is an ideal format to suit the human figure. This of course is not a hard and fast rule, so you are at liberty to experiment and compose your paintings out of the norm.

It is best to avoid placing your main subject, or objects too close to the centre of the composition, or to split the picture centrally, either vertically or horizontally. If this is done your eye will be lead directly to the midpoint in the picture and the rest of the composition will be lost.

When using a rectangular format either horizontally or vertically, the traditional rule to apply is the Golden Mean and also known as the Golden Rectangle or Golden Ratio. This is a principle first devised by the Renaissance painters, who believed it was the perfect layout. It is a format for dividing up a rectangle using geometry, so this principle will help you in designing and structuring your composition.

The Golden Mean is based on the mathematical relationship between three points on a straight line in which the ratio AC: BC equals the ratio BC: AC. A simpler way to explain it would be that a picture should be divided up by a ratio of 2:3. So any important aspect or element within the composition should be placed about two thirds of the way across the paper. This will help to create a pleasing and harmonious picture.

You can use this principle on both the vertical and the horizontal lines, so it is ideal for landscape and portrait viewpoints.

Portable Viewfinder

To compose a picture easier, you can make a portable viewfinder. This is a very practical tool that can be easily made from a fairly thick piece of card about 10cm x 14cm. Cut out a rectangle of 2.5cm x 4cm from the centre of the sheet. To use the viewfinder, hold it away from you, shutting one eye, whilst looking through the aperture at the composition. This will assist you to 'frame' your subject to decide the best viewpoint in which to begin drawing.

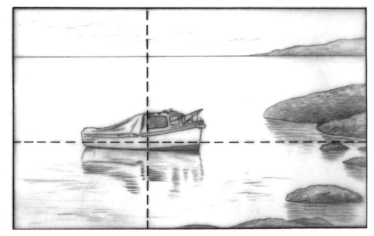

The Golden Mean helps to create the best compositions for your paintings.

With some practice, perspective will create realism into your pictures.

Perspective, the basics

Perspective is an element in drawing that helps to give a sense of depth and realism. If you look up along a straight road, the outer edges of the road seem to converge as they fade into the distance. Where to two edges meet in the distance, this is called the vanishing point.

In fact we know these lines are parallel and do not converge, but the optical illusion created gives us the sense of distance. It may seem complicated to some, but the effect of perspective is relatively easy to produce. Obviously, the more you practice drawing perspective the easier it will become.

Perspective's main elements

Horizon Line

The horizon line is the distant horizontal line which should be roughly level with the observer's eye. The line will change position as the observer changes also, for example if you look at the line from a sitting position and then change to a standing position.

View point

The direction of where the observer is looking will determine the viewpoint.

Vanishing Points

Drawings with perspective will have at least one vanishing point, usually on the horizon line. There are three vanishing point perspectives, Parallel, Oblique and Aerial perspective. These three types are related to the number of vanishing points within a composition.

- Parallel perspective is when all the parallel lines converge to one point.

- Oblique perspective is where there are two vanishing points on the horizon line. This perspective creates two sets of converging lines which meet at their respective vanishing points.

- Aerial perspective is different to the other two types in that the vanishing point can be above or below the horizon line. When used along side oblique perspective, the two types will give the subject in a composition an illusion of height or depth.

Parallel perspective exercises.

As there is only one vanishing point in parallel perspective, start with this one first to get an understanding how perspective works. Refer to the box in the illustration as a guide. Notice all the parallel lines converging to a single point.

- Draw a similar box several times and try changing its width and height.

- Having done that, attempt the two illustrations of the room using the same principle as the box. See how all the vertical and horizontal lines are parallel to the edge of the paper, the same as the box. Only the parallel lines that recede are affected. A little later try also moving the vanishing point along the horizon line.

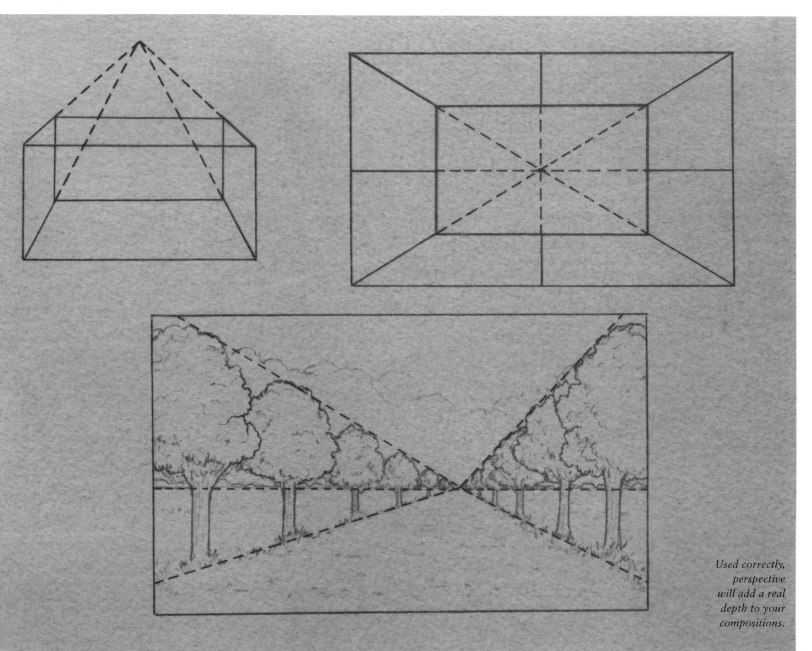

Used correctly, perspective will add a real depth to your compositions.

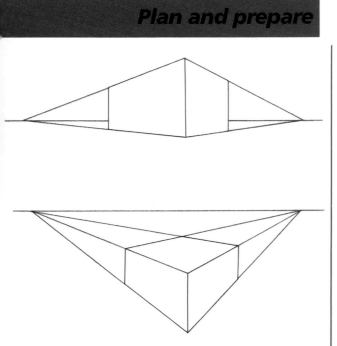

The optical illusion of perspective helps the artist to pull the viewer into the picture

Oblique perspective exercises

When using oblique perspective, you can draw subjects which are placed at an angle. This is most useful when painting buildings, as most often they are at different angles to each other.

• Start with a box similar to that in the first exercise. Place two vanishing points on the horizon line. Draw your guide lines from these points to create the lines which converge at the front edge of the box.

You can change the viewpoint of an object with oblique perspective.

Try, distant, close-up, high and low view exercises.

• If the box is in the distance, it will appear a lot smaller with less sloping of the sides, as opposed to a box that is much closer.

• When the vanishing points are close to the subject on a normal horizon line, the object will appear very close. This is called 'foreshortening' and the sides of the box will seem quite distorted.

• A low viewpoint is when the horizon line moves down the box. This makes the converging lines above the horizon appear steeper.

• If the horizon line is moved up above the subject, this will create a high viewpoint looking down on the subject.

• When a third or 'aerial' vanishing point is added, a sense of height is given to a composition. This works well with drawings of tall buildings.

Further ways of creating perspective

Tone and colour will also create a sense of perspective and will be explained later in the book.

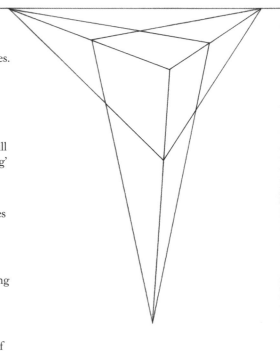

113

For the very best results, it is essential to have the right equipment. Experiment with as many materials as you can to see which type you enjoy and benefit from the most. This practical guide will assist you in understanding the tools and materials available to you.

A Practical Guide

Watercolours

Watercolours are easy to recognise as they are usually translucent colour 'washes', which have a luminescent and delicate quality. They are very useful in capturing the effects of light which makes them highly suited for landscape painting.

One of the main techniques to learn is how much diluted paint you should apply to the paper surface. Once dry, watercolour paints can sometimes appear insipid and pale, but when mastered you can create beautiful spontaneous paintings.

Paints

The ingredients for watercolour paints are coloured pigments mixed with Gum Arabic and Glycerine. They are available in two grades, artist and student. The artist grade has finer pigments of a higher quality and the student grade is less so, but more economical and perfect for beginners.

- Watercolour paint comes in two forms, in tubes and pans. Tube paint is a thick concentrated liquid which is squeezed out and thinned with water.

- As tubes are rich in pigment, these are best suited for work that requires a higher concentration of colour.

- Pans are semi-dry blocks of paint which are usually supplied in a box, but colours can be purchased separately to replenish existing ones used up. There are two sizes of pan colours, full pan and half pan, of which the latter is most commonly used. If painting outside, take a box of pan watercolour paints with you. They are easy to transport, fairly inexpensive and have a huge range of colours.

- Student grade colours being more economical and inexpensive are best suited for beginners to experiment techniques with and gain confidence.

Brushes

Good brushes are very important in painting pictures, so only buy quality ones as cheap brushes do not perform well and last only a fraction of the time as the good ones. It is a false economy to go for the cheaper option, better to buy two really good brushes that last for years, than lots of poor brushes that wear out quickly. There are many sizes available but a beginner will only require three or four brushes, small (size No.1), medium (size No. 6) and large (size No. 14). Perhaps a flat brush could be added to the list at a later date, for larger washes of colour.

There are several types of brushes available for watercolour painting.

- Brushes made from real hair such as Sable, Squirrel and Ox hair, with Sable being the best quality. There are some excellent synthetic brushes as well, which are worth trying out. Brushes come in various shapes and sizes but you will only need a few to start with.

- Round brushes are shaped to a fine point which allows for detail work when the tip is applied to the paper surface. They can also be used to apply a wash, depending on the size of the brush, when swept sideways across the painting surface. With that technique you can apply large amounts of colour as you go.

- Flat chisel-shaped brushes are best suited for laying washes over larger areas. The flat brushes with rounded ends are known as 'Filberts' and fan brushes are also very useful, especially when painting grasses.

- Always wash out your brushes thoroughly when you have finished painting. Shape them back to a point and dry them with the bristles pointing upwards. Never leave them in the water pot facing down or stored in the same manner, as this will damage the point on the brush and so will not work as efficiently in the future.

Painting Equipment

For mixing your watercolours you will need a palette. Boxes with pan colours usually have a palette provided, or you can buy a palette separately from most art retailers. Alternatively, another option is a clean white plate which can be used and then washed after use.

Water pots with screw-top lids are a must if you are painting outside. You will need two, one for washing your brushes and the other for clean water to mix with your paints.

A sketching pencil and a putty rubber are essential tools for drawing your initial guidelines prior to painting. These are explained in more detail later on.

Papers

- Watercolour papers come in many different types and are available in pads, books and as single sheets. They are graded according to weight (gsm, or grams per metre squared), which determines the thickness. These papers are usually rough in texture which allows the watercolour to key to the paper.

- An absorbent paper will soak up the pigment, whereas a shiny paper will not accept the paint readily. Good quality cartridge paper is ideal for watercolour sketching, but do not get it too wet as it will buckle with excessive water. Proper watercolour paper is the best for most paintings.

- Hot-pressed paper is a smooth surfaced paper, whereas Rough paper is heavily textured. Cold-pressed papers are a mixture of the two and are most commonly used.

- Textured papers are essential for watercolour painting as the paint requires a pitted surface in which the pigment can sit. There are various grades of textured paper which will give very different results.

- 300gsm paper is good for most painting mediums including pencil washes, watercolour and also pen and ink.

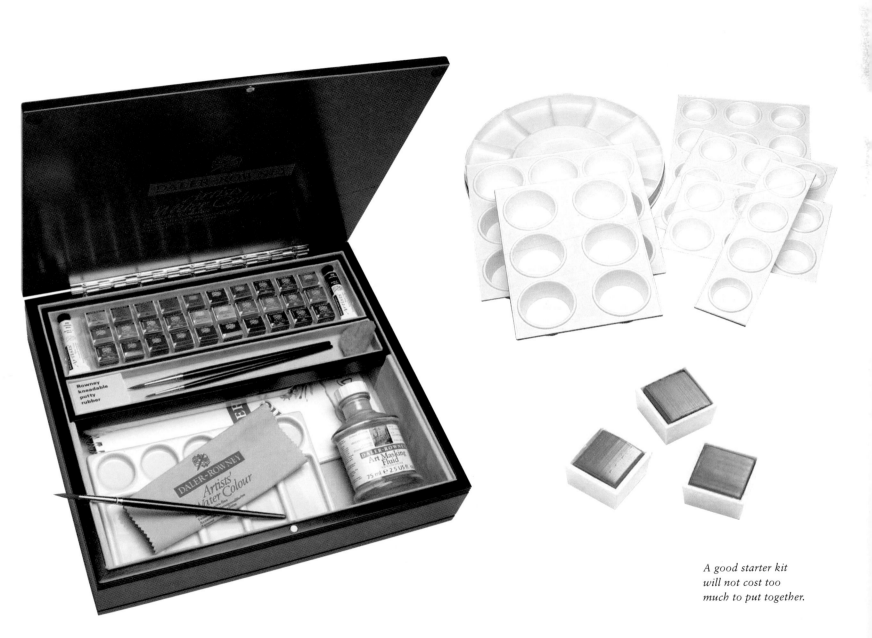

Rowney
kneadable
putty
rubber

DALER·ROWNEY
Artists'
Water Colour

DALER·ROWNEY
Art Masking
Fluid
75 ml ℮ 2.5 US fl.oz

*A good starter kit
will not cost too
much to put together.*

Acrylics

Acrylic paints have only been around since the 1940's and were originally only available in tubes. They have the look of oil paints but are very different, in that they dry very quickly and are water based. You can use them as you would watercolour but once dried you cannot re-work the paint, but you can put other colours on top. You can also paint in thick layers as you would with oils and the picture would be dry in only a fraction of the time that oil paint would take.

Paints

Acrylics come in two grades, student and artist quality. The student grade is perfect for beginners and is economical, whereas the artist grade contains finer quality pigments. They are totally waterproof once dried and so several layers of colour can be achieved without disturbing the initial paint underneath. The paint is now available in two forms, tube paint and a more fluid type in pots. The acrylic in pots is best used for watercolour style pictures and also for fine detail work. The tube colours are more suited for the thick 'Impasto' style techniques.

For beginners, most manufacturers provide starter kits of a few basic colours and are ideal to experiment with.

Acrylic paints are normally thinned with just water, but you can add different mediums to the paint such as Gloss or Matt medium, which will create different effects. Gloss medium will help to make the colours more translucent and will increase the surface sheen to the final picture. Matt medium will also make the colours translucent, but the dried finish will be matt or a slightly more 'satin' finish if mixed with the gloss medium.

Brushes

Acrylic paint will dry hard on the brush if it is not washed properly. For most beginners it is a good idea to start with a couple of cheaper brushes, until you get used to the acrylic paints. Synthetic brushes are good for acrylic painting and the soft round ones are best for the more fluid painting techniques. For thicker layers and 'impasto' style work, use the short flat brushes.

- For covering large areas, use two large flat brushes, one stiff and one soft, the stiff brush to apply the paint and the soft one to blend the colours.

- Use soft bristled round brushes for detailed work and stiff bristled brushes for applying thick layers of paint.

- Try also experimenting with a palette knife for heavy 'impasto' work made up of colour straight from the tube.

- Always remember that acrylic paints dry very quickly and are waterproof when dried, so keep your brushes moist whilst working and clean them during and after painting.

Tools and Equipment

A ceramic palette is ideal for mixing acrylics colours in and if you already have one for your watercolours, you can use that for your acrylics too. You must wash the palette out thoroughly when finished to remove any dried paint. Paper palettes are excellent for mixing acrylic paint on as each page on the palette is disposed of when finished and so cuts down on the mess.

A palette knife is a useful tool for mixing thick paint and for creating 'impasto' effects.

Papers and Boards

Acrylic paper can be purchased in pads, but acrylics can be painted on to any surface such as thick paper, card, canvas and hardboard. If the surface is too porous or un-primed, you will need to apply a coat or acrylic primer called gesso.

Oils

The most traditional painting medium throughout many centuries has been oil paint. It dries slowly which allows the time to experiment and if necessary time to correct or alter the painting.

Oil paints can be mixed together wet-in-wet or applied onto a canvas in layers, with each layer being allowed to dry first. It can be used very thick, either with a stiff brush or with a palette knife in an 'impasto' style.

Oils can also be thinned down with turpentine or linseed oil to create a more fluid medium, which is ideal for detailed work.

Paints

Oil paint is made from colour pigment mixed with linseed oil. It comes as a thick paste in tubes and is available in a large range of colours. Starter kits of student grade colours are available for the beginner to try out.

When oil paint is thinned with turpentine it produces a matt finish when dried, but when linseed oil is used it creates a glossy finish.

If mistakes are made, the wet paint can be scraped off or rubbed with a rag dipped in turpentine. If the paint has dried it can be painted over with ease as the paint is opaque enough to cover any unwanted areas.

Brushes

It would be advisable to buy inexpensive brushes whilst learning to paint in oils, but don't go for the very cheapest as they may lose their bristles and shape easily. A selection of shapes and sizes of bristle brushes would be a good start to experiment with.

Soft round brushes are best for the more fluid style techniques and the short flat brushes are good for applying thicker paint layers.

For large areas use two large flat brushes, one stiff and one softer brush, about 2.5cm wide. For detailed work use a soft, thin round bristled brush.

Experiment with a palette knife for applying thick 'impasto' layers of paint straight from the tube.

Tools and Equipment

A palette for holding and mixing your paint is important and these can come in many forms. The traditional palette is made of wood with a thumb hole. A china or enamel plate would be adequate, as would a piece of hardboard. The disposable paper palettes are ideal as they can be thrown away when finished.

Cotton rags are essential for cleaning and wiping brushes, palettes, hands and canvas throughout the painting process. A rag dipped in turpentine or white spirit will remove any unwanted paint whilst still wet.

Keep your cleaning and thinning mediums, such as turpentine and linseed oil in old screw-top jars.

Keeping your brushes clean is essential.

121

Painting surfaces for oils

The traditional surface for oil painting is canvas or wood but beginners could start with oil or acrylic paper. Stretched canvas or canvas boards are available in many sizes and varieties. Hardboard or medium density fibre board (mdf), coated in at least two coats of gesso or white emulsion are good surface alternatives.

Gouache paint

Gouache paints are similar to watercolour and were first used by 14th century monks in their illuminated manuscripts. It is an opaque paint and is made from pigment mixed with chalk and gum arabic. It has a matt finish as opposed to the translucent quality of watercolour. Another difference is that white gouache can be added to lighten a colour, as opposed to thinning down watercolours to let the white of the paper show through. Gouache paints are water-soluble and can be used in a similar way to watercolour, so you can use the same equipment.

Storing your materials

A plastic tool box from a DIY store is an excellent storage solution for your art materials. It is light, robust easy to clean and has a carrying handle.

A good art folder is another essential piece of kit as it can store your loose papers and drawings. They come in a number of varieties and prices, so check them out at your local art supplier.

Papers

There are many different papers for the artist to choose from and come in many forms. They are available in book form such as sketch pads and individual sheets. Paper is graded by its weight (gsm, or grams per metre squared), which determines the thickness of the paper. It is available in a huge range of colours and textures. Some papers are textured to produce certain effects when painted on and some suit certain materials. Other papers are more universal and used with a wide variety of different materials.

It is worth experimenting with different papers to see what can be achieved and suits your needs.

- The smoother papers are good for pencil sketches and detailed compositions created in pen and ink where the lines appear clean and fine. Cartridge paper is the good all rounder of papers and is often used in many sketchbooks as the ideal paper for this purpose. Very smooth papers are the hot-pressed papers which give a hard, unforgiving line whereas the cold-pressed papers are a little more textured producing softer lines.

- Textured paper is the ideal paper for watercolours as it well suited to produce different effects from the various grades. There are some very coarse grades and others not so much, which give soft, rich tones.

- Oil and acrylic paper pads can be purchased cheaper than canvas or board and are more cost-effective.

Things to look for in the weight of paper:

- 150gsm is good for drawing and sketching.

- 180gsm being heavier in weight is more suited for soft pencil and charcoal drawings.

- 300gsm is ideal for watercolour pencil work, line and wash and for general mixed media compositions.

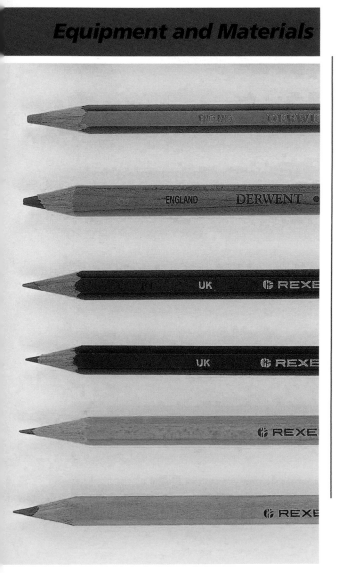

Graphite Pencils

The 'lead pencil' as it is often called is in actual fact made of graphite and come in varying degrees of hardness from 9H to 8B. Pencils are incredibly versatile and the most commonly material used for sketching and drawing. They are portable and also very cheap to buy with many brands available. Mistakes are easily rubbed out with an eraser or putty rubber and can make a seemingly endless array of different marks.

- When grading pencils, H indicates 'hard'. H pencils are best suited for technical drawings due to the hard grey marks that they make. They can indent the paper and are often difficult to erase when mistakes occur.

- B pencils are 'soft' pencils and are the most widely used pencils for drawing by artists. They produce darker, softer marks and are easily removed with an eraser. These types of pencils are also easier to manipulate, blend and smudge as well, creating a varying range of tones.

- Good quality pencils are always the best to use as some cheaper alternatives may damage your painting surface and possibly give uneven marks. A good set of pencils will include a 2H pencil for detail drawing, an HB for basic work and note taking, a 2B for drawing and sketching and a 4B and a 6B for darker tones and heavier shading.

Other types of drawing material to consider are graphite sticks which are made of pure graphite and used in the same manner as pencils.

- Wider strokes and marks can be achieved when used on an angle.

- Sepia sketching pencils are a brown pigmented pencil, traditionally used for sketching a subject on to a canvas. Used on paper it produces a pale brown line which is easily smudged and water soluble.

- Sanguine sketching pencils are richer brown pencils and are also used for drawing on to a canvas. Often these pencils are used on coloured paper with white chalk as highlights.

Watercolour pencils

Watercolour pencils are a mixture of pigment and clay and all sorts of effects can be created with these soluble pencils. The pencils at first are applied in the normal manner and then water is added with a brush to create a watercolour wash effect. Dry pencil work can be added on top once the water has dried to create various textures and tones. Use them in a watercolour composition to produce a mixed media painting.

Pens

The first pens used were simply sticks dipped in to ink which progressed later on to feather quills to allow a more fluid, constant line. For the artist today there is a vast array of different pens and markers to choose from.

Some are still being used with dipping ink or cartridges and others have their own built in supply.

Some water soluble ink pens can be used with water to produce great watercolour effects. This will soften lines and block in subtle areas of tone. Ink from these pens can sometimes be spattered, blobbed, stippled and sponged to create interesting and varied effects.

Accessories

- The putty rubber is a soft malleable rubber ideal for lifting off pigment from paper and canvas. It will remove lines and tone whereby you can create highlights. It is can also be shaped into a point by hand to remove small areas of pigment. Being soft, these rubbers will not damage a painting or drawing surface as a harder eraser might.

- Erasers are harder rubbers and best suited for removing pencil marks from tougher papers. Take care not to rub too hard as they may damage the paper surface.

- Paper stumps or 'torchons' are pencil-like strips of rolled paper which can be sharpened and reused. They are used to blend pigment together with greater effect than a finger.

- A drawing board is basically a piece of board used to clip or tape your paper onto. This will ensure it will not slip about whilst you are working.

- Pencil sharpeners and craft knives are essential tools for sharpening your pencils. Craft knives are particularly useful as they sharpen pencils, cut paper and boards. The tip of the knife can be used to scratch into the paper to create highlights and lift away pigment for unusual effects.

Rowney
kneadable

Rowney
kneadable
putty
rubber

Large

Basic equipment

These are the very basic items you should have regardless of the style of painting you are working on. Use these items with any of the suggested materials from the previous sections in the book.

• Pencils, 2H, HB, 2B, 4B and 6B.

• A putty rubber and harder eraser.

• A spiral-bound sketchpad and a bound sketchbook.

• A craft knife and pencil sharpener.

• Paper tissues or soft rags for wiping off paint and cleaning.

• A roll of masking tape for securing work to the drawing board.

• A wooden or metal easel if required.

Learning to See

As a beginner you should spend a lot of time drawing, observing and really looking at a variety of different subjects. Planning and creating your compositions such as still life, portrait and landscapes from direct observation. Learn to see the world through new eyes.

Learning to see is a skill like any other and this is something that every artist has to practice and master. The easiest way to do this is to break a subject down to its various components, form, tone, colour, texture, etc.

- Practice looking at how things relate to each other to help you compose good paintings. For instance, look around your room and breakdown the items in your eye-line into basic shapes. Observe the way those shapes relate to one another and do they overlap? How are they grouped together and where is your eye naturally drawn to? Could this be made into an interesting composition? Once again look at the same subjects, but think about tone, texture and colour.

- Experiment with your subjects in two different ways, objective and then subjective as previously mentioned in the book. First, take a look at your object, person or view in a very analytical way, to be able to represent this objectively in a composition? Think about what you see and how you can recreate this. Then begin to imagine how the subject makes you feel, to start thinking about representing it in a more emotive and subjective way.

- Take into account that all objects, spaces and subjects can change according to various factors such as time, light, mood, etc.

The subject may dictate the medium or style of painting, or drawing you wish to produce. Think of the practicalities for instance, if you are sketching skies or a busy market place on holiday. Pencils, pens or watercolours would be ideal to capture the essence of the subjects and are very portable. Still life subjects could be produced in oils or pastels with plenty of time for drying and fixing.

- Think about your objectives and what the composition is about.

- Is it going to be a sketch, research material or a finished composition?

- Will it be objective or subjective and how can you communicate your perception of the subject? Take into account the previous exercises and how you can relate them to your aims for a particular picture.

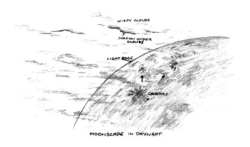

WISPY CLOUDS
SHADOW UNDER CLOUDS
LIGHT EDGE
CRATERS
MOONSCAPE IN DAYLIGHT.

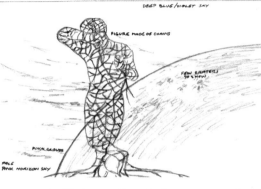

DEEP BLUE/VIOLET SKY
FIGURE MADE OF CHAINS
FEW CRATERS TO SHOW
PINK CLOUDS
PALE PINK HORIZON SKY

- Attempt all manner of different subjects as the more you draw and the broader your subject knowledge, the quicker you will begin to develop your own style. Understanding many subjects will assist your imagination to inventing your own compositions, but you do need to have a basic technical knowledge to turn imagination into art.

- Develop your hand-to-eye coordination and remember to allow your own interpretation of the subject to help shape your composition. With enthusiasm, even though you would be thinking of the technical aspects of the work, you should be halfway there in creating a visually stimulating composition.

Do your research, make visual notes and plan your imaginative painting, there's no need to create a masterpiece the moment you sit down.

Developing Skills

Sketching a few minutes each day will improve your eye-to-hand coordination, allowing you to attempt ever increasing challenges in techniques and compositions. To become an artist, to think and view the world the way an artist does, requires patience and practise.

Many artists spend a lot of time practising techniques and collating information in their sketchbooks, for developing their compositions. These are often a great source of material that they have either drawn or collected for use at a later date.

The best way to progress as an artist is to keep a sketchbook that you can practise in every day. Treat it as an exercise, so the minimum of 15 minutes per day will keep you in trim artistically.

The Sketchbook

The sketchbook is basically an artist's aid and is an essential piece of equipment. It can hold all the information that you would need in the form of drawings that you produce, notes and details of various subjects within it and cuttings for reference.

When buying a sketchbook consider how big it is. Too big a sketchbook will not transport so easily and can be quite awkward to work with on a location. However, it should be big enough to hold all the information you wish to gather comfortably. A consideration is to have two books, one small sketchbook for your pocket or handbag and a larger one for home studies.

Your sketchbooks should be made of cartridge paper in a spiral-bound pad or hardback books. However, if you prefer to work in ink, watercolour or pastel, then you may wish to purchase a sketchbook that suits those particular techniques. For general drawing and note taking, a basic sketchbook will do for that purpose.

How to use your sketchbook

Your sketchbook should not be a finished composition, but a personal visual and technical aid. It is for your development and confidence without fear of judgement, as you can make as many mistakes in it as you wish. Practise some sketches without the use of a rubber and that way you can see any mistakes you have made. You can refer back to them later when you draw that subject again.

- Practise new techniques in your sketchbook to hone your skills, everything from small individual studies to lines and textures.

- Also within your sketchbook, try working out and practising the rules of perspective or attempt new subjects. Try different mediums and techniques or even invent new ways to mix certain mediums together. Some will work, while others will not but you will learn a lot from trying.

- One of the crucial sketchbook functions is to act as a reference point for more finished compositions. Record such details as tone, texture and colour with any other information that will have an influence on the final composition. View and draw your subjects from different angles to help you visualise them more clearly, in finalising the structure of your pictures.

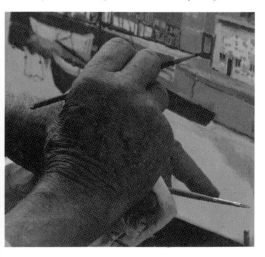

Hone your skills by practising in your sketchbook.

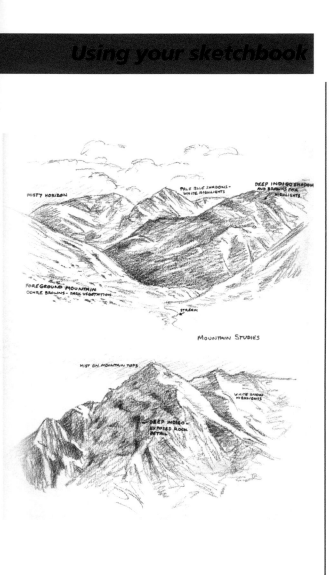

MOUNTAIN STUDIES

Sketchbook exercises

- Choose a subject such as a fruit or a view from a window and draw it at least four times or more, over a period of a week. The more times you draw the subject, the more you begin to understand it. You will see how your interpretation changes on the later attempts and you should find your sketches becoming more fluid.

- You can try limiting yourself to a time scale in which to produce a quick sketch of a simple subject. Start at two minutes each sketch and then decrease the time until you reach a time of 30 seconds per sketch. This will speed up your sketching ability and will make you concentrate on just drawing the essence of the subject. Don't worry too much about drawing detail at this stage.

- A good exercise for your sketchbook is in knowing what to paste into it as reference. Don't get too carried away as the book will become too bulky, but do paste cuttings from magazines, photographs, bits of fabric, even dried leaves. So long as these items are useful as reference for later paintings, or spark an idea for a composition.

- Try a limited use of colour, what's known as 'limited palette'. Use maybe only three or four colours in a composition or when colouring a sketch.

- Experiment with different drawing or writing tools to explore what types of marks these will make. Some interesting ideas and drawing

To capture the essence of the subject, try the one or two minute sketch.

techniques can be achieved by using items such as ballpoint pens.

- If your subject has lots of exciting qualities for example, good texture or tone, form or colour, then make several sketches of each in turn.

- Create an abstract interpretation of an everyday object to be able to break it down to its simplest form. This will help you in capturing the essence of a subject.

- Repeat these exercises over and over again with different subjects, materials and colours. Try to do at least two or more a week to keep you artistically 'fit'.

aste images in the sketchbook to inspire you.

LICHEN STUDIES

STRUCTURE OF LICHEN

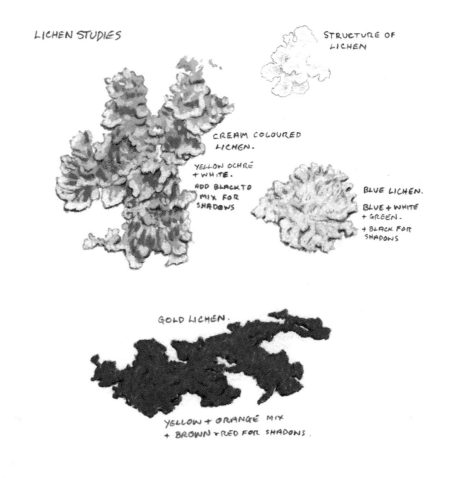

CREAM COLOURED LICHEN.

YELLOW OCHRE + WHITE.
ADD BLACK TO MIX FOR SHADOWS

BLUE LICHEN.

BLUE + WHITE + GREEN.
+ BLACK FOR SHADOWS

GOLD LICHEN.

YELLOW + ORANGE MIX + BROWN + RED FOR SHADOWS.

Sketchbooks on field trips

An important function of your sketchbook is to be a portable studio, so whilst out you can easily capture elements of particular interest. Many artists find inspiration when they are out on field trips and amongst nature and also everyday scenes. If you are out and have your sketchbook and pencils handy, you can make quick sketches to use later in developing a complete painting.

Keep a sketchbook to hand at all times whilst out as a subject will grab your attention when you least expect it, or you can pre-plan a field trip to gather reference material.

If you are planning a reference gathering trip, you should make some basic preparations to ensure the whole trip was worthwhile.

Planning field trips

Here are a few basic steps to consider when organising a field trip.

- Be prepared for the weather, in some places it can be unpredictable, but this is what adds drama and makes good pictures. However, take a foldable raincoat if it is likely to pour down and some refreshments. Dress appropriately as you will not feel like sketching if you are too hot or too cold.

- Carry your art materials in a sturdy bag such as a rucksack, as you may have to travel quite a distance to reach a certain location to sketch.

- A quality waterproof bag will last for years and protect all your equipment.

- Carry a diverse range of sketching materials, to capture different aspects of a subject. Remember to also take a bottle of water for your watercolours and water-soluble pencils.

- Materials you will need are a craft knife to sharpen your pencils, a rubber and a clean rag, selection of brushes and paper clips to stop your paper blowing in the wind.

- Some artists take a small collapsible stool to sit on, but a plastic ground sheet will suffice as it is easily transported and fairly light.

- When you are working in the open landscape, you will find that you are not in control of the subject or the surroundings. Also the light will be constantly changing, which will obviously affect the shadows. This means you will have to work faster than you would in your home surroundings and learn to sketch quickly.

- Don't waste a lot of time on detail or elements you can add later and make a few notes to accompany your drawings to help you later on.

- Focus only on the essential information of the subject and choose the materials that will help you to achieve that goal.

- If you are unable to sketch your chosen subject, try a different source for reference. If it is a view whilst on holiday for instance, perhaps a postcard or a magazine article may help you in creating a composition.

- Bear in mind not to copy those references exactly for copyright reasons and also they should only be a starting point or inspiration for your paintings.

- If you are sketching animals or people, they have a habit of moving around. The best way to approach this is to keep drawing the subjects in different positions then you can rework them as they return to each of those positions.

Photographs and Notes

You can support your sketches with photographs or notes on your subject to act as reference or an aid, to help you in the development of the composition. If your sketches are drawn in pencil or charcoal, you can use the photographs to provide colour information or the notes to describe the quality of the light which sometimes photos cannot capture.

- Use your photographs to give you different compositional viewpoints.

- An overall reminder of a subject or scene is useful when creating a final painting.

- When photographing your subject, capture specific elements such as colour, form and close-ups of textures for reference later.

- Subjects such as birds flying are difficult to sketch

but easier to capture with the use of a camera and then used as a basis for a finished painting.

- Photographs should be a starting point for most compositions and not relied on as the only source of reference. Sometimes if you just copy a photograph the resulting picture could be dull and lifeless.

Making location sketch notes will help in remembering the scene or subject. You can write some of these notes next to your sketches as an additional reference. Simple notes or bullet points will help you to cross-reference your drawings and photographs much more easily.

Field Studies

- Sketch a view from different viewpoints and with different mediums, over a period of several visits. You should start to really get to know the scene and once you have done this, attempt a composition from memory, capturing the essence of the subject as opposed to the technical details.

- For wildlife field studies, try very quick sketches to create a more fluid representation, containing the basic elements of the subject. Captive animals in zoos, nature reserves and wildlife parks are a great place to study different species of animals. Concentrate on the overall proportions and posture and don't get too bogged down with details at this stage.

- For flowers or trees, try sketching them over a period of a few weeks to see how they change and alter according to the seasons. Study how

the weather and different light qualities changes their appearance and also how decaying plants can produce interesting shapes and textures.

- When choosing a theme such as trees or buildings, gather as much material as possible in the form of sketches, photographs and magazine clippings. Always be on the lookout for interesting examples of your subject whilst on your travels.

- Always have your sketchbook handy when you are on holiday. Different countries can provide new subjects for you to tackle with a vast array of stunning landscapes, wildlife, buildings and people. Many of these subjects will inspire you, so make plenty of notes and sketches to allow you to create interesting compositions when you return home.

- Sketch a scene at different times of the day to see how the shadows fall and the tonal values change. The early morning light quality will be totally different to that at dusk.

- Sketching from life will give your compositions a firm foundation of form and structure. Knowing how a subject moves or grows, changes according to light or weather conditions, will help you to interpret your subject with far more clarity.

The following chapters contain exercises for you to practice in your sketchbook. These will be a continuous record of your progress as an artist.

Lines, Tone and Texture

How to hold your equipment is one of the most important things you need to learn before you make any marks. You must learn some basic drawing skills before you start to paint, as you will need to support your paintings with research sketches, as well as drawing guidelines of your subjects on your paper or canvas.

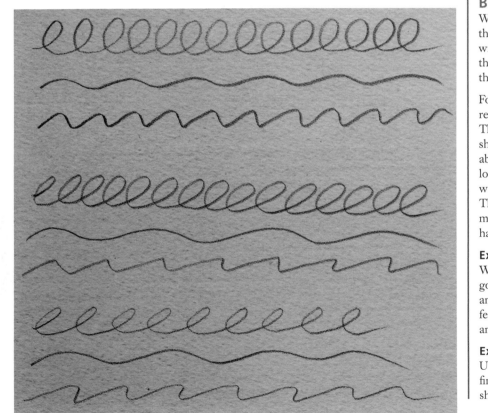

Exercise 1

Exercise 2

Exercise 3

Basic Drawing techniques

When holding a pencil most people grip it near the drawing point then move their fingers and wrist. This produces a tight linear control much the same as writing. There are other ways to hold the pencil when drawing.

For the more artistic way, hold the pencil lightly, releasing the tension from your fingers and wrist. The drawing action should now come from your shoulder and through your elbow, with the wrist absorbing some of the action but still remaining loose. Holding the shaft of the pencil further up will affect the marks that you choose to make. The higher up the pencil your fingers are the more fluid and loose the line. Avoid resting your hand on the paper if you can whilst drawing.

Exercise 1

With an HB pencil, hold it as though you were going to start writing. Now draw the looped, wavy and zigzag lines as illustrated. You will find that it feels rather restrictive drawing with a tense hand and wrist.

Exercise 2

Use the same pencil, but this time move your fingers up the shaft and repeat the exercise. You should find this action a little more fluid in your wrist and the motion should come from your shoulder.

Exercise 3

Once again repeat the exercise, but hold the pencil shaft even further up. Allow the pencil to travel lightly and smoothly across the page by really moving your arm as you draw. The lines will now look very free and spontaneous. By comparing all three exercises, you will see the difference of how changing your hand position on the pencil will affect the marks that you make.

Exercise 4

Using the techniques from exercise 2, draw the looped circles as illustrated. Concentrate on keeping the line evenly spaced, continuous and fluid.

Exercise 5

In drawing it may seem as though there are unlimited types of lines and marks to make, but in fact there are four basic styles of line to use.

The illustration of the four boxes demonstrates how an object can change according to its linear quality. The four types of lines are:

• Wire line, a clean and constant line which you would use for sharp definite outlines.

• Calligraphic line, as an uneven and variable width line, it is useful for emphasising tonal qualities.

• Broken line, this being a short line is used repeatedly to convey a more subtle outline.

• Repeated line is a free flowing, fluid style of line which has an organic quality. It is a series of loosely parallel lines which form a built up outline.

Draw the boxes in the various styles of line then try circles or even irregular shapes to get used to applying the methods to other subjects.

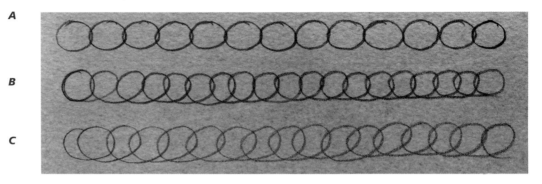

Exercise 4

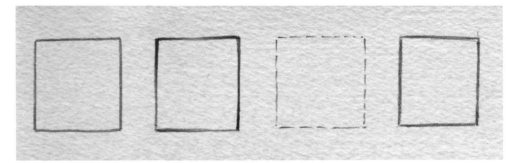

Exercise 5

With lots of practice you should now be more confident in using graphite pencils and the effects that can be achieved by simply altering the amount of pressure, type of stroke and hand position. Keep practising the different techniques to ensure you become more confident in the use of these basic marks. They are the foundation of any composition and the basic skills you require.

Having grasped the basics of handling a pencil, now you can begin to explore other mediums. The following exercises will assist you in learning how to apply paint to make interesting marks.

Basic Watercolour techniques

Watercolour paint is a delicate medium so fluid and gentle strokes are required. Use flowing strokes with the brush and keep your grip relaxed.

You will be able to make a wide variety of lines and different marks depending on the size of your brush. Use the tip only for detail and three quarters of the brush pressed to the paper for wider strokes. Any more pressure and you will wear the brush away.

Use a No.6 brush for the following exercises as illustrated.

- Paint a line with the tip of the brush.
- Apply more pressure to create a thicker line.
- Wipe excess paint off the brush to make an uneven and broken 'Dry Brush' line.
- Try using a slightly thicker paint and the tip of the brush once again.

- Practice a curved line with a more fluid paint mixture.
- Draw with the brush, try the three sided box and fill in with colour.
- Experiment with a range of different marks and try various water and paint mixes.

The following marks can all be made using the same brush which can add texture to any painting. Try dragging the brush with a dry brush technique or stippling and dotting with the tip, or using thick and thin lines.

Flat tone wash

A fundamental element of watercolour painting is the 'wash' technique. It is used to cover large areas with colour.

- For this technique use a cold-pressed watercolour paper. It will help if you tilt the paper to a 30 degree angle to allow the paint to flow down the paper, although it is not essential. Use a large (No.6 or higher), soft watercolour brush.

- Mix a small amount of paint with plenty of water in a palette and enough to cover the area. Watercolours tend to dry paler, normally twice as pale as the wet colour so allow for this when mixing.

- Load the brush with the watercolour mix and using a long, broad stroke, paint an even band of colour straight across the top of the paper. You will notice that the paint will collect and pool at the bottom edge.

- Reload your brush again and repeat the process but this time, pick up the excess at the bottom with the second brushstroke as you go. Try not to apply too much pressure on the stroke and let the paint flow naturally.

- If you stop halfway the wash will dry and look uneven, so keep working until you have finished.

- Apply wet paint onto wet paper, or into painted areas that are still wet to produce a wet-in-wet technique. This creates a soft blurring effect which is excellent for painting dramatic skies.

- Paint a graduated wash, in a similar fashion to the flat wash by adding more water to the paint, thinning each stroke down.

- Layer different colour washes together to give a translucent and almost ethereal effect when the colours blend and combine together.

- You can soften edges of painted areas by lifting off some colour with a wet brush. Use a soft tissue to remove pigment and excess paint to create a translucent effect.

basic wash

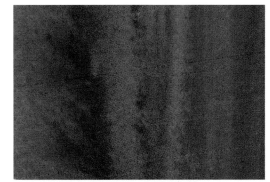
wet-in-wet

graduated wash

layering washes

softening edges

removing pigment.

Making Artistic Marks

Basic Oil techniques

Oil paints can be used in many ways to produce a wide range of different marks and textures. You can use thick round or flat brushes for large areas and thin brushes for delicate strokes whereas, wedge shaped brushes make thick, smooth marks.

Use any suitable oil brush to make the marks as illustrated in these pages.

All of these techniques will be useful in your oil painting and also changes can be made by adding mediums such as turpentine or linseed oil to thin the paint.

- Wet-in-wet (wet paint into wet paint), mix different colours directly on the canvas. Use a fluid paint and brush the layers together.

- To create smooth blends, use soft gentle strokes where the edges of the colours overlap to fuse them together.

- To create stroke-on-stroke effects, apply different colours in rough strokes and allow the paint to remain intact. Do not blend the paint as the colours will look blended from a distance and have a lively appearance close up.

- Use thin lines to add detail or to mix colours in a stroke-on-stroke effect.

- To paint a scumble effect, apply the paint thickly on to the canvas in swirling, fluid strokes with a dry brush, cloth or even a sponge.

- Creating an Impasto painting is where the paint is applied very thick with either a brush or a palette knife. Create a three dimensional composition by painting thick, buttery paint roughly on to the canvas.

- Overlap colours together to create layers by painting in thick strokes.

Smooth stroke

Stroke on stroke

vast array of different textures and strokes can be produced *th oil paints when applying these techniques creatively.*

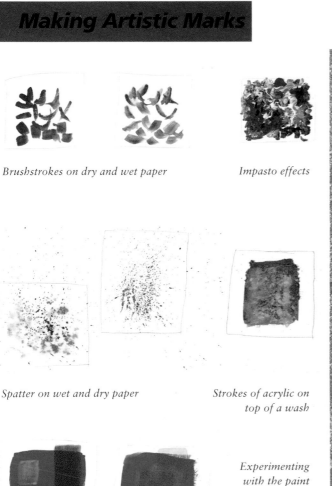

Brushstrokes on dry and wet paper

Impasto effects

Spatter on wet and dry paper

Strokes of acrylic on top of a wash

Experimenting with the paint will help you to discover its potential and feed your imagination.

Translucent wash layers on top of each other

Basic acrylic techniques

Acrylic paints are very versatile and can be use in similar techniques to watercolours or oils, depending on how thick you use the paint. Thin the acrylics down with water to produce translucent washes or use them thicker for opaque brushstrokes. To discover the versatility of acrylic paints, experiment with the following exercises.

• Apply the acrylic paint straight from the tube on to dry paper with bold brushstrokes then try the same onto wet paper to see how the paint reacts.

• Use thick layers of paint on top of each other to create a three dimensional Impasto effect.

• Apply a wash on to paper and allow it to dry. Paint thicker strokes on top to add texture.

• For a spatter effect, thin down some paint and flick the brush with your finger. A toothbrush is also a good tool for this technique and you could try this on both dry and wet paper to see the effects.

• Paint a translucent wash on to paper once again and allow it to dry. Apply another layer of translucent colour on top to see the subtle change of the colours used, which depends on the intensity and depth of the washes.

Basic Tone Techniques

You are now able to begin creating pictures as you have all the basic techniques required. All the different types of marks you have learnt are the building blocks and skills for producing tone and texture within your compositions.

Tone is the degree of light and dark within a drawing or painting and refers to the amount of light which you see when you look at a colour.

Black and white photographs are made up of tones captured by the camera in a single colour, also known as a monotone. Sepia tones are monotone and the colour is generally brown. Think of your subject as though it were a monotone when applying tones to your composition. Recognise where the dark, mid and light tones are situated within the subject and the overall composition.

Exercise 1

- Draw nine squares to produce a tone scale board and colour in the last square black. Fill in the other squares and decrease the tone as you go until you reach the last square which should be almost white. The paper itself will represent absolute white.

Exercise 2

- Copy the simple landscape illustrated by using only three tones from the tone board. Throughout the composition, concentrate on maintaining the three tones consistently.

Exercise 3

- Now use four tones to copy the simple scene illustrated. Apply a varying range of tones and think about how the light will affect the tone. Imagine how a subject's tonal quality would be affected by dark shadows on a sunny day.

Exercise 4

- Attempt a simple tonal still life, like the flowers illustrated. Break the picture down into shades of light and dark and do not worry about too much detail. Areas of light and shade help to shape the objects and create a feeling of perspective, which gives them a three dimensional quality.

Exercise 1

Exercise 2

Exercise 3

Exercise 4

145

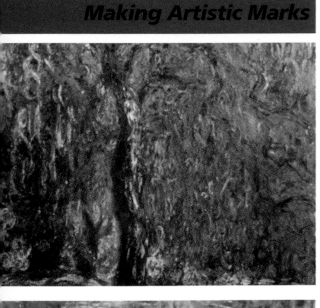

Line, Tone and Texture Exercises

Start making interesting compositions by utilizing all of the previous exercises and using a range of marks to indicate line, tone and texture.

Look at the illustration of the grasshopper painted in acrylics which looks complicated. It is actually made up of three types of marks, dots, circles and straight lines, which give the illustration depth and texture.

Exercise 1

- Draw a simple household object such as the cup shown in the illustration.

- Draw the basic shape and then add tone and depth by simple pencil shading techniques. Now draw the same object using dots to produce the tones.

Exercise 2

- Continue exercise one and now add more detail, tone and texture to the drawing. Experiment with the use of different lines and marks to see how your subject can be interpreted in various ways. The illustration of the three bottles clearly shows different interpretations of the same subject.

Exercise 3

- Sketch many different types of textures as you can find.

The watercolour painting of the nude concentrates on the tonal qualities and form of the figure. Fine brushwork in the leopard painted in acrylic shows detailed texture added on top of block colour. Both landscapes painted in oil using Impasto techniques capture the texture of two different subjects, water and foliage. Dry brushstrokes were used on top of a delicate watercolour landscape, to produce the picture of the tree with dramatic contrast.

- Attempt your own sketches; look closely at plants, animals, trees even bricks or fabrics, anything with texture.

Practice all the exercises until you feel really comfortable with your drawing and painting skills. You will then be ready to compose more adventurous pictures.

With practise you will improve your mark making skills.

The Basics of Colour

Without the proper use of colour, the perfect composition, use of tones and the right mediums will all be made redundant. Studying this useful guide on colour will assist you in making the most out of your palette.

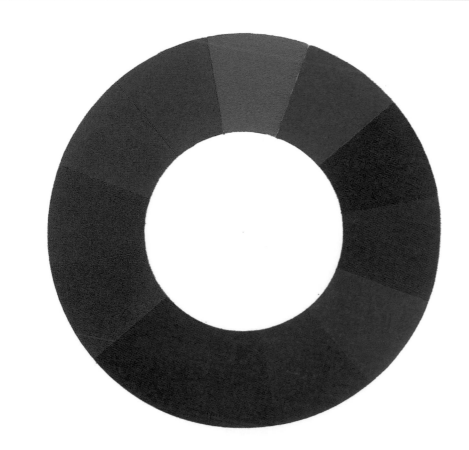

The Colour Wheel

The colour wheel is a visual illustration of the three main qualities that make up any colour. These are hue, tonal value and intensity.

- A hue is the name of a colour such as red, orange, violet, all are common examples.

- Tonal value is the lightness or darkness of a colour. To darken or shade a hue, add black pigment and to lighten or tint a hue add white pigment.

- Intensity is how bright or dull a hue is. The more brilliant and vivid a colour is the stronger the intensity. For example yellow has a strong intensity, whereas violet has a dull appearance due to its weaker intensity.

- The colour wheel is made up of three types of hue, primary, secondary and tertiary.

- Paint a colour wheel in your sketchbook to help you understand more about using colour. Draw a circle and divide it into six equal segments.

Primary colours

There are three primary colours, red, yellow and blue. These colours cannot be mixed from any other colours and are pure and very bright. They are easily recognised whereas other colours or subtle hues are not so easy to distinguish. Paint the colour wheel with the three primary colours and positioning the yellow at the top, as indicated.

Secondary colours

When you mix yellow and red together, you make orange which is known as a secondary colour. Secondary colours are always made from mixing two primary colours. Add yellow and blue to make green and red to blue to make violet. Include these colours to your colour wheel as indicated.

Complementary colours

All primary colours are complemented by a secondary colour, never another primary, for instance red and green are complementary colours.

On the colour wheel, these colours are directly opposite and are visually opposed to each other. Study and use the colour wheel to learn about which colours complement each other. When using complementary colours within a composition, use them sparingly as they will stand out and could appear too jarring to the eye.

Colour mixing with black

The colours in the example from the colour wheel have been mixed with black, which has given them the appearance of being shaded. They now look duller and darker in colour.

Tertiary colours

Tertiary colours are made up of a primary colour mixed with a secondary colour. For instance, yellow – green, red – orange and blue – violet. These are all examples of tertiary colours and placed on the colour wheel between each related primary and secondary colour.

Colour mixing with white

The colours in the example from the colour wheel have been mixed with white, which has tinted the colours. They now have the appearance of being a softer colour and much lighter.

Colour to create mood

Good use of colour can convey a sense of mood within a composition and initiate an emotive response from the viewer.

If you look at the two photographs, both are of still water scenes, but the mood in each of them, because of the colour is quite different.

The picture of the boats is predominantly blue in colour and is a tonal value composition. Because of the colours, it is cool, serene and almost unnerving in its calmness, which also gives a sense of emptiness. This is reflected beautifully in the empty boats, which appear to be abandoned.

The photograph of the sunset edging into night is a scene of solitude and yet it still appears warm and inviting. The golden yellow tones radiating across the sky and reflected in the water have warmed up the whole scene.

These examples show how important the correct use of colour can be when creating a composition. Use the colour wheel to help you select the appropriate colours to convey the moods you wish to produce.

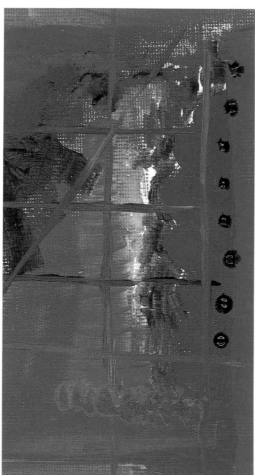

Warm and Cool colours

If you were to draw a line through the colour wheel, from the yellow down to the violet, you would separate the two halves into warm and cool colour palettes.

The warm colours would be the reds and oranges, think of sunsets, fire or the sun. Whereas the cool colours would be the blues and greens, think of the sea or ice for blues and lush cool foliage for the greens.

A mixture of both warm and cool colours can be used in a composition; however, some striking effects can be achieved by using just warm or cool colours. The abstract paintings illustrated were each produced with colours from one side of the colour wheel. To show how a subject can appear different according to the colours chosen, the pears were painted in warm and then again in cool colour palettes.

For a balanced composition, use a mixture of the two types of colour palettes. The photographs of the bowl of apples and bananas seem cold and lifeless in the composition when in purely tonal colours. The yellow image is lifelike and warm whereas, the predominantly violet and green images seem to be quite stark.

This is something to bear in mind when showing highlights or shadows.

For example, if you are painting a tree, you can add yellow highlights and blue shadows to accentuate form and structure. You can also convey a sense of depth by painting warm colours in the foreground and cooler colours in the background.

The mood of an image can change dramatically by the use of tonal colours as the three pictures clearly illustrates.

153

Light and Dark colours

Depending on the tonal values used, a painting can be seen as light or dark, just as it could be viewed as warm or cool.

Most paintings have specific areas of light and dark, which can warm and forward or cool and recessive. By adding white to lighten or black to darken a colour will have a cooling effect on the colour it is mixed with.

If you are going to add white to a colour, start off by mixing tiny amounts of colour to the white paint. This is much easier than trying to lighten an existing colour and it will save you lots of paint in the process. A thing to remember is that most white in a painting will be tinted by another hue.

Another way to lighten or darken a colour is to add a colour which is close to the colour you wish to change. This will change the hue without cooling it down.

The watercolour still life painting illustrated, is a light painting because the white of the paper was allowed to show through the pigments and in effect lighten them. Now the painting has a translucent, delicate look to it. In contrast, within the painting of the Cougar, a lot of the colours have been darkened to make the cat appear that it is in shade and give the rocks a heavy and solid look to them. However, the sunlight on its coat is much brighter so white and a little yellow was added to lighten the colours.

C. Christoforou.®

155

Working on a still life composition is the best way to progress from sketching to creating more adventurous pictures. These types of paintings will benefit you in setting up compositions that you have total control over, from the positioning of the subject to the lighting conditions.

Still Life Composition

Composing your Still Life

As you begin to tackle more complex compositions, as opposed to drawing simple sketches, it is best to start off still life studies.

With this type of picture you have total control over your working conditions and you can take your time, without the concern that it will move or change dramatically. It is wise not to attempt anything too complicated at first, so set up a simple still life with two or three basic shapes and colours.

If your still life is positioned near a window for the light source, you should bear in mind that the light conditions will change. A better alternative is to use an angle poise lamp which is easy to control and can be directed at the subject. The still life will now receive the exact amount of light and shadow required.

The shape of the subject will dictate whether your composition will be landscape or portrait format. As an example, a tall vase of flowers is best done as portrait, whereas a selection of scattered fruit is best painted in a landscape format. The illustrated oil painting of flowers and fruit is a good example of this.

Decide on the style of painting you wish to produce. Will it be a subjective composition, by capturing the abstract qualities of the subject? Or will it be objective, with a more accurate view of the subject matter, which will be a representational picture. The watercolour painting of the peach and banana illustrates this well.

You should try to make your compositions as exciting as possible, so observe the objects well to arrange them into interesting positions. The six illustrations of simple still life studies are examples of how to arrange the subjects within a composition.

Shapes such as circles work best when there is a variation in size.

When not in a straight line, the bottle, circle and box form a more interesting composition. In the final example, the objects are grouped together as this is a better way to compose a still life, rather than all the objects being spread out evenly. Try and use a variety of different forms, heights and sizes to add extra interest.

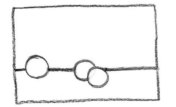
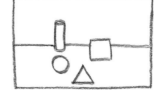
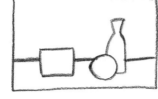

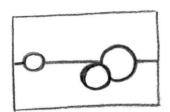
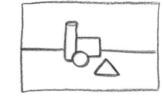

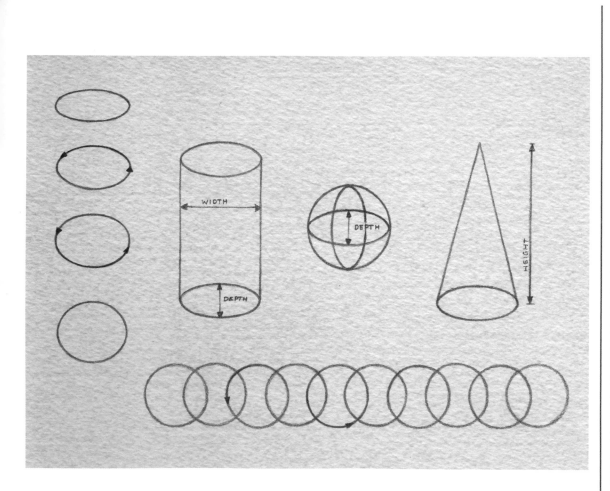

Drawing rounded objects

When creating a still life composition, you will discover that many of the objects you wish to draw contain circles or curves. The simplest way to draw any rounded object is to break it down into one of three basic shapes, cylinder, cone or sphere. You would then add the detail once you have drawn the basic form.

Take a look at the top of a glass, plate or bottle from straight on and you will see it appears to be flat. However, when you tilt it forwards, you will notice that it is rounded. This flattened circular shape is known as an ellipse.

Practice a simple ellipse by drawing a flattened circle. Use a 2B pencil very lightly so you have a smooth motion. Repeat the exercise several times and gradually flatten the circle a little each time. This will help you to get the feel for different shaped ellipses.

Drawing circles may seem difficult, but if you keep your wrist relaxed and draw with your whole arm, you will get better the more you practice.

Don't press too hard on the pencil, so any mistakes you make can easily be rectified with an eraser.

Now you can try drawing the three main shapes, cylinder, cone and sphere.

For the shapes to appear three dimensional, practice varying the depth of the ellipses. If you are under-drawing or over-drawing the shape of the ellipse, you will notice that the object looks distorted. With practice you will be able to draw the ellipses at the correct depth.

Axis lines

To help you draw rounded objects much easier, use the axis lines to get the correct angle of the ellipse. Getting the right angle is important especially if the object is tilted.

The upright line indicates the height (or length) axis and the horizontal line is the depth (or width) axis.

Once you have drawn the height and width axis, you can then start to draw in the circle or ellipse. Try to draw each quarter section as a mirror image to next.

When drawing objects such a glass or bowl, you will need two horizontal axis lines to create two ellipses, one for the top and one for the base. The illustrations clearly show examples of this. Even when the object is at an angle, the ellipses must be parallel to each other, or the object will look distorted.

Try drawing the shapes shown in the illustrations then draw some of your own.

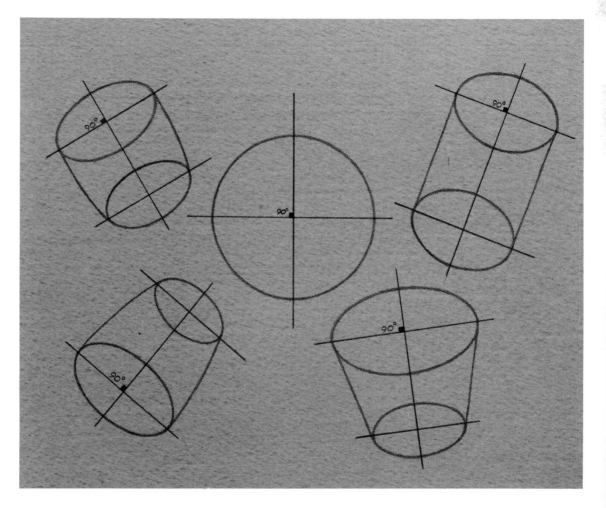

Objects as simple shapes

If you look at the illustrated still life, you will notice that the objects within it can be broken down into easy to draw simple shapes. Continue on from the cylinder, cone and sphere method, to breakdown more complex three dimensional objects.

Practice breaking down objects into simple shapes as they will be much easier to draw. Start adding detail once you have captured the basic shape of the object.

Draw fairly lightly with the pencil when sketching in the shapes, so any guidelines can easily be removed.

Always remember to draw a central axis line so you can arrange the ellipses along it. You should still do this even when the object is at an angle.

Notice how an ellipse is shallower and rounder at eye level, than one which is above or below eye level. Remember this when looking at your shapes.

When you are drawing objects that are close together and some parts are obscured and you cannot see them, this does not mean that those parts are not there. Bear this in mind when positioning your objects close together in your composition. This will ensure the depth of the composition is not distorted.

Light and Shade

An extremely important element of still life painting is the use of light and shade and the effects it creates among the chosen subjects. The illustrations clearly demonstrate how the light source can change the look and feel of a still life. By placing the light source in front of the subjects, extreme contrasts of light and shade are possible.

However, when the light source is positioned above the subjects, the composition creates quite a different effect. This is now far more exciting tonal composition which gives a feeling of solidity. This is a better way of lighting a group of objects. It now creates a sense of drama between the various shapes, especially through the intensity of shadows.

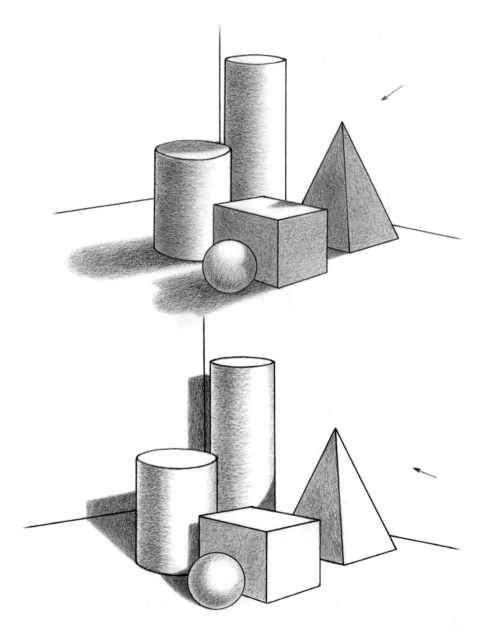

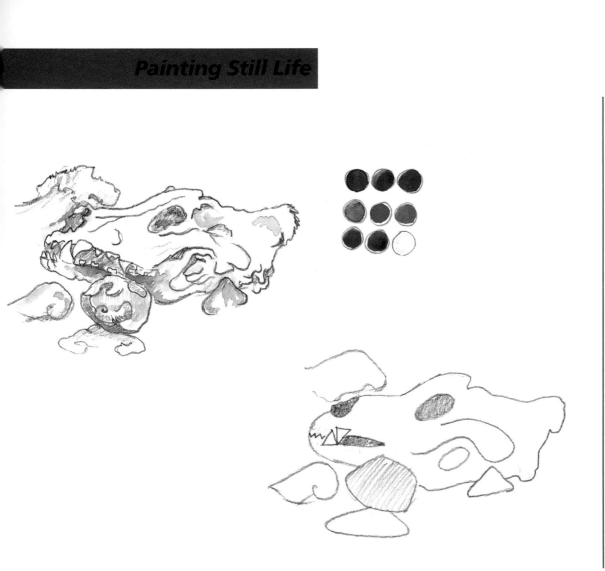

Still life – Example 1

A lot of people think that a still life painting is about flowers and bowls of fruit. In fact still life paintings can be created using any objects that excite you to paint them. The composition illustrated proves that an exciting painting can be produced from a wide variety of different subject matter. The objects in the picture are of a skull of a dog, surrounded by fossils, bones and shells.

The composition is not in a formal or stuffy format, but rather in a more fluid and relaxed fashion. The brush strokes are free and vibrant even though the subject is observational. The use of light and colour is a little more subjective. The main focus is on the skull, giving a sketchy feel to the remaining objects.

Do not feel that you have to capture every detail in the subject, as some of the best compositions are successful when they are not over worked.

Learn to give your composition space and concentrate on the necessary elements that you wish to express emotion and meaning.

- **Step one** – Break down the objects in the still life into basic, simple shapes.

  If drawn lightly, the working-out pencil lines can be erased as the more detailed sketch is completed. Keep the shapes very light and simple to start with. This means that if required, the position of some objects can be changed without having to erase detailed drawings.

- **Step two** – Start blocking in the basic tonal elements of light and shade with a No.6 brush. As the medium is watercolour, it is important to remember to work from light tones first then to dark tones. This is known as light to dark. Once a dark pigment is applied onto your painting, you cannot paint over it with a lighter colour.

Keep your colours to a minimum, you should use cadmium yellow, cerulean blue, ultramarine, burnt umber and raw umber, violet and white. Overlap simple washes of colour to produce different tones.

- **Step three** – Finally, add detail to the painting by including a few darker areas which you can pick out using a charcoal pencil. This will add depth and definition to your composition. You can leave much of the outer area un-worked to allow the skull to remain the focal point of the picture.

Still life – Example 2

This example of an oil still life is a simple and traditional composition. The elements have been kept to a minimum to create more focus on the two subjects and not too much distraction around them. As it is a simple design, only a few colours have been used and these are medium yellow, cerulean blue, magenta, violet and titanium white. Experiment a little with the colours initially, to give you the results that you want to achieve later on your composition.

Step one – Block out the basic shape in a flat tonal colour and leave the very pale areas white. Lightly pick out the darker shadowed areas on the rose and then use a little thinned down paint on the bowl.

Step two – Use white with a little colour added, to scumble the background to give a softer and more delicate feel. Pick out the highlights on the leaves with a little yellow and reflect that onto the surface of the bowl.

Step three – Finally, add some detail to soften the whole composition.

For instance, add texture to the petals of the rose and richer tones on the tablecloth. Use more buttery tones on the bowl to finish off the entire composition.

Composing a landscape

A certain amount of organisation is important when attempting a landscape painting. Creativity is crucial in making a landscape interesting, but there are several structural elements to consider before getting down to the composition.

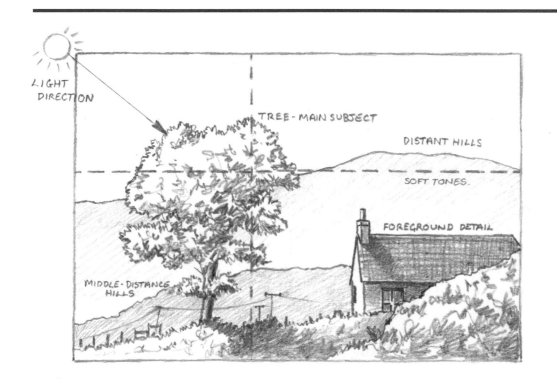

LIGHT DIRECTION

TREE - MAIN SUBJECT

DISTANT HILLS

SOFT TONES.

FOREGROUND DETAIL

MIDDLE - DISTANCE HILLS

When you are attempting a landscape painting on location, you will have to factor in environmental influences such as the weather and the changing light conditions.

• Make a note on the position of your light source, such as in most cases the sun, or the moon or streetlight if you are working at night. In the field sketch illustrated, you can see the position of the light source, in this case the sun. From this position the highlights and shadows can be worked out where they will form. When the light changes and it does outside, you will have a basic reference point to work from.

• For your composition, use the Golden Mean principle to divide the basic areas up. This will help to ensure that your main subject is not positioned too centrally, which will later detract from the rest of the picture.

• Taking notes in your sketchbook will help you to remember certain details that you may need later. They will also ensure consistency throughout the composition.

The more a composition breaks the rules, the more effective it will be, so don't be afraid to experiment and think 'outside of the box'. The two paintings shown of the reflected trees clearly illustrate this point. They both divide the space up in a very linear and almost abstract way.

Everyday scenes can be rendered in abstract and intriguing ways, but do your homework first before embarking on a difficult piece.

Background elements and Skies

Many artists base a lot of their landscape work on particular elements of this type of painting, such as skies, water, sunsets or mountains. These are all crucial background features in landscape composition.

The landscape painting of a prehistoric theme is dominated by a foreboding dramatic sky. The lines of clouds however echo the prone skeletons of the extinct dinosaurs. A most effective feature is the use of yellow to highlight the stormy blue-grey clouds.

In complete contrast, the basic watercolour of a tree and hills is a delicate, bright and vibrant picture. In fact this painting was produced by a 6 year old boy. It is very effective even though everything is kept simple and representational.

The semi-abstract mountain scene illustrated, was produced by experimenting with salt onto wet acrylic paint. This was done in order to create a sense of torrential rain.

- You should have a go at painting a variety of skies and water effects, either separately or within the same piece. Be spontaneous as the best effects are those you least expect. When you are painting natural looking skies or water scenes, try not to over-work them. You can use the following examples to help you.

Sky techniques

- For portraying a calm summer sky, try a graduated watercolour wash.

- Use wet-in-wet washes to create a cloudy sky effect.

- In a predominantly white sky, you can paint small areas of colour to represent the gaps in the clouds.

- Dramatic sunsets can also be created using the wet-in-wet technique.

- A restless stormy sky can be created by scumbling oil paint on the canvas or board.

- Very convincing skies can be painted in oils when applied smoothly, especially when a few wispy clouds are painted in by dragging white paint across the surface.

Water techniques

- By scumbling watercolour paint, you can create a sense of rough seawater.

- Pick out reflections by using dashes of colour and leaving the white of the paper to act as the reflected light on the tips of the waves.

- Blend lines of paint together to give the illusion of lapping water.

- Scumble, drag and splatter oil paint to create waves and spray.

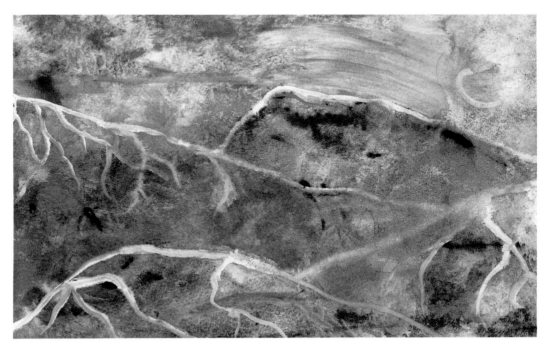

Trees and Flowers

Most landscapes that you see will contain some kind of greenery even industrial areas usually have some kind of wild plants growing on them.

When painting trees or flowers, texture is vital because it helps to give the illusion of movement in leaves or delicate flowers. Texture is crucial when painting rough bark.

The landscape oil painting conveys this well, as the trees seem to be gently moving thanks to the delicately textured foliage.

The lilies, also painted in oils, possess a quality of natural light and movement and yet are not particularly observational in content.

The Slipper Orchids however, are painted in acrylics and are more stylised with the use of rich colours and thick paint, to create a sense of tropical opulence.

For future reference material, draw and paint several observational sketches in your sketchbook. Make them fairly simple and practice drawing many different types of plant life.

For the successful depiction of trees and flowers in your compositions, practice and master the techniques of creating texture.

171

Drama and intrigue can be introduced into a painting by the proper use of perspective.

Buildings

For the beginner, buildings can seem to be a daunting prospect to tackle, because they are technically more complex than a natural object. The best technique for making this subject easier is to leave out any unnecessary elements and only include the important aspects of the buildings. This technique will give you a sense of the building without getting overtaken by technicalities.

The following paintings show various interpretations of how to portray the linear qualities of different buildings, whilst still remaining fluid and interesting.

- There is little detail in the sketch of the street in Prague, but the sense of perspective ensures that your eye travels up the street. The buildings seem to bustle with the interesting architectural elements.

- There is an even greater indication of the importance of perspective in the oil painting of the church. As it is very foreshortened, it highlights its importance in relation to the figures within the painting.

- The lack of detail and form in the picture of the haystacks and misty scenes, all convey an impression of structure without the need to overwork the composition.

- Finally, for other elements that may require a more linear approach, these can be interpreted in interesting and fun ways, such as the sketch of the fence post or the illustration of the car.

Animals

There are so many incredible and beautiful animals out there, that it is no wonder so many people choose to sketch and paint them. Animals can often be hard to capture on paper, either because they move around a lot or sometimes due to their complicated anatomy. To make the process easier, you can break the animals down into basic shapes, as shown in the illustrations of the dog, cat and horse.

You can practice drawing proportions from still images such as photographs, but always try to see your subject in its natural environment where possible. This will give you a greater understanding of how it moves and generally behaves.

Your quick sketches may not be anatomically correct at first, but the more you practice, the more you will be able to capture the spirit of the subject.

- The small drawings of the cat jumping have very little detail and yet have caught the movement of the leap.

- The sketch of the cow with its calf has captured the gentle nature of the subject.

- The horse sketch painted in oil, has concentrated on the subject's demeanour.

- When drawing and painting animals, it is essential to sketch as much as possible in your sketchbook to act as reference material. Always try to capture and convey the animal's essence and spirit.

174

Landscape – Example 1

Try painting this very simple composition of a small cottage and lots of trees, in watercolour. You will only need to use four colours in this painting, phthalo blue, deep yellow, hooker's green and payne's grey. You will also use the white of the paper to show through for the cottage walls and for highlights.

Step one – Use an H pencil very lightly to sketch in all the elements of the composition. Start painting in some light colour washes into the sky area. With a mixture of blue and grey wash, paint into the areas of shadow.

Now begin to place the areas of green wash, into the background, the sky and the roof of the cottage.

Step two – Mix Hooker's green with water and then the other colours to make a range of tonal greens. Begin to form the trees by applying these mixtures to the background, keeping the strokes fluid and use plenty of water.

Step three – You can start to add little areas of detail, such as the tree trunks and shadows under the trees. Now darken out the windows, but do not over work the painting as it should be very free and tonal. There should only be a little detail in this painting, as it is all about practising your wash techniques and mixing tonal colours from a limited palette.

Step one

176

Step three

Landscape – Example 2

You will need your oil paints for this composition of the woodland water scene and a No.5 medium flat brush and a No.2 round sable brush. There are only four colours to use to create a range of tones and these are titanium white, ultramarine, burnt sienna and cadmium orange.

Step one – Sketch in the composition and then begin painting by blocking in the main tones. Now you can blend in the sky with white and blue. Then proceed onto the mountains, keeping them fairly light to give the impression of distance. Paint in the darkest areas which will be the foreground as this is closest to you, then add in the mid-tones for the trees and water.

Step two – Start adding a little detail, such as the foliage on the tree and the reflection on the water. With a smooth and even stroke, use a fairly dry brush for the reflection.

Step three – Now add in the ripples on the water with the small sable brush. With the tip of the bristle brush, darken the shadows in the two fir trees and then thicken the foliage on the main tree. Finally, pick out a few highlights with a mixture of cadmium orange and white.

Step one

Step two

Step three

Proportions of the Figure

Throughout history the human figure has been featured in paintings, including those on cave walls by early man. Before the age of photography, the only way to record an image of a portrait or the full figure was by painting it. You can be part of that history by learning how to paint and draw portraits and the human figure.

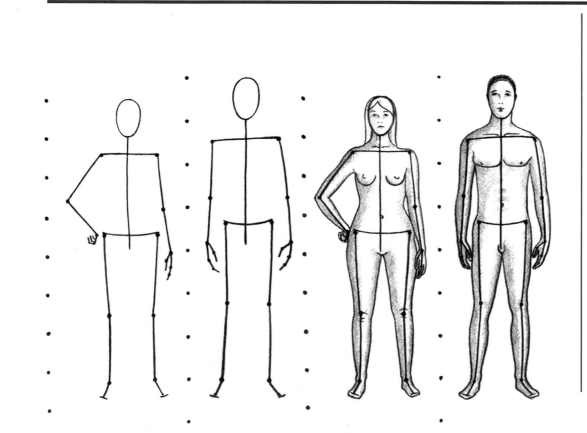

For creating realistic and proportionally accurate figures, here are some guidelines to help you understand how to draw both male and female figures. The method to use was first invented by the Renaissance artists and is still the most common method today. Look at the stick figures of the man and woman and then at the fully drawn figure, you can see how to apply the one to the other.

- No two figures are the same, but there are some basic guidelines for you so you can judge the correct proportion.

- Use the head as a unit of measurement, where the 'average' male would be approximately 7.5 heads high. In taller people however, they would be around 8 heads high.

- The torso section of the figure, from the chin to the pubic area, is normally 3 heads tall. You can divide the torso into equal thirds, from the chin to the nipple line, then to the navel, then to the pubic area.

- The distance from the upper leg to the knee is approximately 2 heads in length and the lower leg is also the same length.

The width between the shoulders in a man is around 3 heads wide, whereas a woman's shoulder width is about half a head less.

From the top of the head to the elbows is roughly 3 heads in length. When standing upright the wrists would be approximately parallel to the pubic area. However, this would change according to the pose of the figure you are drawing.

The female figure is slightly smaller than the male and you will notice that the hips are usually the same width as the shoulders. This can measure around two heads or a little more.

Try to capture the character of the person you are painting as well as getting a good likeness. However, your paintings do not have to be exact copies of photographs to create interesting portraits of people.

Proportions of the head

When beginning to think about painting and drawing portraits, you have to start with structure. As with all art subjects, it can take a while to master, but with practice you will find drawing and painting portraits exciting and very rewarding.

The basic design you can use for a head is one that is oval shaped, with the tapered end at the bottom and the neck can be just a simple cylinder. This basic shape can now be divided into rough proportions, which will give a stylised version of a human head and features. It is important to remember that every face is different, so you will have to practice and experiment to master the

techniques of getting a good likeness.

- Start to measure out the head by dividing the oval shape into halves, both horizontal and vertical. The two horizontal halved are then divided again to create four equal segments. The eyes are located on the central line which divides the oval in half. The distance between the eyes is the same length as one eye.

- The eyebrows are about a quarter of the distance above the eye line, so draw this in as a faint guide line.

- The nose and ears are placed in the segment from the eyebrow line to the baseline below the

centre. The mouth is around one third below the nose to the bottom of the chin. You can draw another faint guideline for this as well.

- With these guidelines you should be able to sketch in the basic features of the human head in proportion.

At this stage the head is neither male of female, but bear in mind the differences such as, a woman's features are softer and less defined than a man's. The older the person, the more pronounced the features become and children tend to have smaller noses and mouths, but comparably larger eyes.

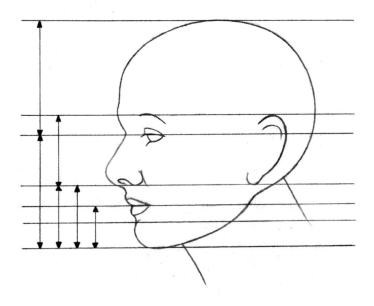

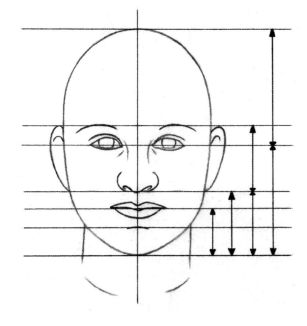

Portraits and Figures

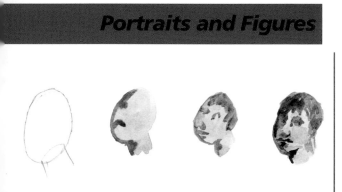

Portrait and Figure details

To build up your confidence in painting figures or portraits, you should practice making lots of quick sketches of different parts of the body and face. It is always best to work from life if possible, preferably if you can get someone to pose for you or just sit in a crowded area to sketch the people around you.

You will find that the rules of proportion are altered slightly by the way a person is sitting or standing. The human body is affected by different positions, so careful observation is called for, particularly when you draw a figure close up. Just as in still life or landscape drawing, the body is affected by the rules perspective. One aspect of this is the figure closest to you will seem proportionally larger than a figure further away.

With plenty of practise you will gain your confidence to attempt more complex poses.

The step-by-step examples on the following pages will help you to try out the various elements of portrait painting such as eyes, noses, mouths and ears. Start by drawing the subject in to basic simple shapes then you can add the detail, once you are happy with the proportions and position of the features.

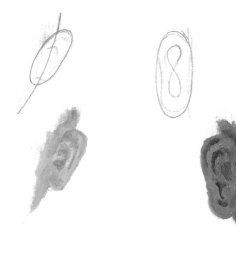

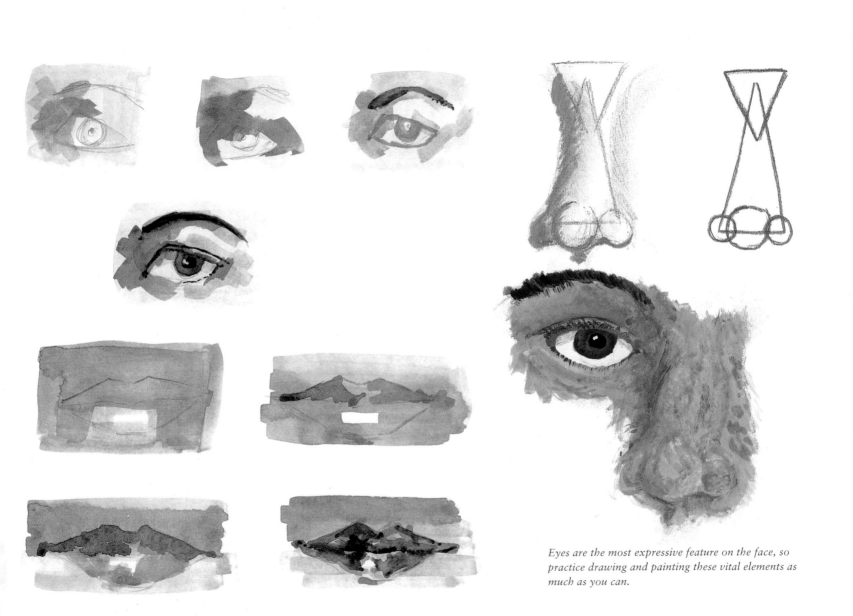

Eyes are the most expressive feature on the face, so practice drawing and painting these vital elements as much as you can.

Figure – Example

You can try this very basic watercolour figure study. Use a limited palette of colours, burnt sienna, Payne's grey, yellow ochre and medium yellow. You will also need a No.6 sable brush.

Step one – Start by very lightly drawing in your figure in basic shapes. Once you are happy with the results, start painting by applying a wash of yellow ochre around the figure. Now block in the initial areas of shadow with a very watered down Payne's grey.

Step two – Paint in the figure with very translucent washes of colour, but leave the paper to show through for the lightest areas, these will be the highlights. Build up the tonal areas with wash-on-wash layers.

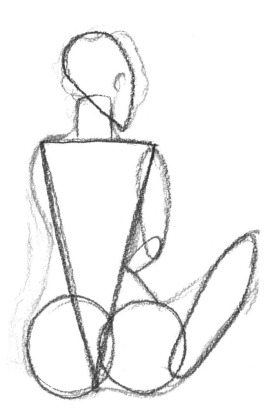

Step three – Finally, add less watery, darker washes of burnt sienna where the shadows are strongest. This will give the figure a sense of form and add perspective to the composition, which will help the figure to stand out. If there are any areas that appear over painted, you can lift off the excess colour from the paper with a clean wet brush.

Portrait – Example

The following step-by-step example of this young girl is a little more complex. You will need a more extensive palette of colours such as, yellow ochre, terra rosa, burnt sienna, raw umber, cobalt blue, violet and titanium white. This is a good exercise in layering tones to create accurate skin colouring and shadows. Keep experimenting with mixing flesh tones until you feel that they are what you are aiming for. Allow plenty of time for each stage to dry before re-working the picture. This painting can also be produced in acrylic, where the drying time is a little quicker and easier to work on top of existing colours.

Step one – Begin by sketching in the girl's face with yellow ochre and burnt sienna for the darker areas. For the flesh tones, use a mixture of yellow ochre and terra rosa, with varying degrees of white. Pick out the cooler flesh tones in cobalt blue. Use cobalt blue and violet for the t-shirt.

Step two – You can soften the skin tones by using lots of tinted white and blending them together. Make the tones deeper in the hair and darken the eyes with raw umber. Pick out some details such as the eyelashes.

Step three – Finally, you can add more work to the background to soften it then brighten up any highlighted areas to contrast with it. With a mixture of cobalt blue and raw umber, paint in the iris of the eyes and pick out the highlights. It is at this stage, where it is a good idea to leave the painting for a short while and come back to it later with fresh eyes. That way, any discrepancies will be more apparent and can be rectified to finish the painting.

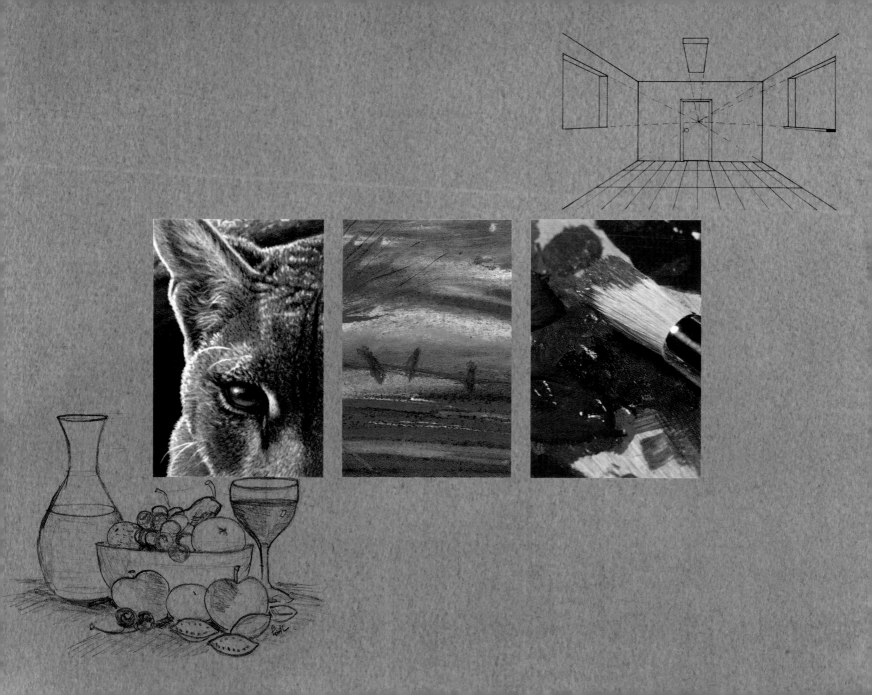

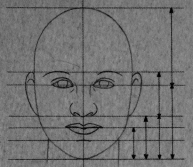